THE CHURCH
AND THE
URBAN CHALLENGE

THE KNUBEL-MILLER LECTURES — 1961

The Church
and the
Urban Challenge

By

Walter Kloetzli

BOARD OF PUBLICATION
OF THE UNITED LUTHERAN CHURCH IN AMERICA
PHILADELPHIA

© 1961 BY MUHLENBERG PRESS
Library of Congress Catalog Number 61-14757

Printed in U.S.A.

UB899

To

CAROLYN

RANDY

BILLY

NANCY

PREFACE

Within the relatively limited format of this lecture series I have included as comprehensive a picture as possible of the contemporary challenge called urbanization, together with a delineation in depth of some of its particular aspects and correlates. In addition, I have declared what I believe to be some key issues facing the American Protestant church. By way of illustration I describe some types of response that have taken place in recent years, both in the Protestant church and in the Roman Catholic church where it has come into conflict (*not* just competition) with the Protestant church.

It may seem repetitious to some readers that I choose to preface these lectures with a brief statement of why the church should be concerned with urbanization. Unfortunately, far too many church members and pastors seem not to have appropriated some basic facts about both the mission of the church and the condition of the society in which we live.

First, it must be pointed out that such concern rests on a biblical foundation. Both the prophetic voices of the Old Testament and the missionary voices of the New Testament ring with the affirmation that God's Word is meant for all nations and all creation. Those who would limit the scope of acting in accordance with the Word to the mere proper behavior of a select group of privileged individuals are condemned. Those who bear witness to that Word are enjoined to go out into the world, *as it actually is,* and bring the Grace of God to all people. There is, then, no biblical restriction placed upon the area of the church's work—it is everywhere. Nor is there any question of the church restricting itself to answering the "spiritual" needs of people—the Bible reminds us again and again of the Christian's concern with the *total* man and his *total* needs.[1]

It is plainly evident that, to a varying extent, the American Protestant church has been failing to minister to the total society in which we live. Ours is an urbanized society, becoming increasingly urbanized, and, barring a major catastrophe, will never again be a rural society. For the most part, American Protestant churches have been fleeing from the seething turmoil of the modern city and have sought refuge in the relative security of the quasi-pastoral suburbs. Where they have remained, geographically, within the city life, they have tried to maintain a rural frame of reference— a "village" atmosphere—thus forming "pockets" that have lost touch with the ongoing life of the real city.

Clarification is necessary here, to distinguish between the urban and rural frames of reference. Rural life is characterized by "primary" group relationships, and urban life by "secondary" group relationships. It means this: primary group relationships are those based on *love,* as within the family, between close friends, and so forth; secondary group relationships are those of the larger community in which a close personal relationship of love cannot exist but for which *justice* provides the basis.[2] As America has shifted from a rural to an urban society, the importance in people's lives of the primary relationships has decreased proportionately with the increase of the importance of secondary relationships. In the more informal and personal rural society, the two kinds of relationship tended to be almost coterminous, thereby making it easier for the dynamic of the love relationship to influence the broader com-

[1] For a thorough discussion, see *Christian Social Responsibility,* ed. Harold Letts (3 vols.; Philadelphia: Muhlenberg Press, 1957).

[2] The two types are sometimes known as *Gemeinschaft* and *Gesellschaft,* after Ferdinand Tonnies, Max Weber, and others.

munity (although the latter still operated on principles of justice, rather than love). Today, however, urbanization has brought about a situation in which these two relationships are quite distinct. It is exceedingly difficult for the "community of love" to surmount the ever-rising bastions of the "community of justice." Indeed, at times it may even seem impossible.

In the past, the church had only to direct its message to primary group relationships to make its influence felt in the wider community. Today it must direct its efforts toward the individual and his immediate relationships—but it must *also* enter itself, consciously and humbly, into the wider arena of the community of justice. It must join in the fight for justice. If it does not, it will be an ineffectual witness to God's Word in our time—in effect, it will be writing off a large segment of God's creation in order to nourish the sanctification of a small group, and even this latter may have less to do with the Word of God than with the perpetuation of a hopeless status quo. In my opinion, the failure to recognize this situation can only mean that the church will fail to make its message relevant to urban life—the life of today, and of tomorrow.

There may be legitimate difference of opinion how to go about making the Christian gospel relevant in our time. Certainly there are a variety of techniques that can be used in such an effort. But there can be no argument, it seems to me, about two things: first, that we are living in a particular kind of mass society that can only be called "urbanized"; second, that, although the Christian gospel is changeless and eternal, human beings are not, and thus this gospel must be made relevant to every age, including our own.

Under these basic assumptions the following lectures were delivered.

—WALTER KLOETZLI

TABLE OF CONTENTS

1

THE URBAN UPHEAVAL

What is the "urbanized" society? How does our contemporary society differ from that of a few decades ago? And in what direction is this society moving? These are the questions the church must ask, and answer satisfactorily, if it is not to be an "ostrich" institution in today's world. These questions are under constant surveillance by our social scientists, and, therefore, before we can look at the place of the church in the urbanized world, we must heed the results of their search and research.

These first two lectures are thus primarily derivative and didactic, perhaps even repetitious to some readers—but for the large percentage of our pastors and laymen, the information they set forth is needed for an understanding of the whole subject.[1]

METROPOLITANIZATION

Anyone who reads the newspapers and magazines (or even watches television) has come across innumerable references to the growth of metropolitan areas and the shift in our population away from the rural scene. Some of this material is carefully researched and thoughtfully presented, some perhaps is incomplete and misleading. This section is based on a research monograph coming out of the Urban Land Institute in Washington, D. C., which is an excellent, up-to-date analysis of urban trends.[2]

[1] For supplementary material, see Walter Kloetzli and Arthur Hillman, *Urban Church Planning* (Philadelphia: Muhlenberg Press, 1958).
[2] Jerome P. Pickard, *Metropolitanization of the United States* (Research Monograph 2, Urban Land Institute [1200 18th St., N. W., Washington, D. C., 1959]), pp. 8, 43.

Our "great" cities, according to this report, had already begun to emerge in the nineteenth century, for in 1900 the New York metropolitan area had a population equal to that of the entire United States in 1800. However, the twentieth century is really the age of metropolitanization as we define it today, for in 1900 there were only four metropolitan areas with a population of one million or more, only nineteen with a population of 250,000 or more—and only 21 per cent of the country's total population was found in these areas.

Obviously this situation has changed considerably in the last sixty years, statistically and in other respects as well. The city has expanded rapidly: geographically in the "urban sprawl," culturally through our new communication media, industrially, and even vertically, as the skylines of some of our cities testify. Politically, the metropolitan area is today anything but a solid bloc; as the outlying areas are integrated with the city's economy, they remain politically fragmented.

This evolution of the city has been "dramatic," to say the least, but what should concern us is what the future promises if the present rate of expansion continues. Here we must return to the statistical approach.

> By the year 2000, with normal population growth, the United States may contain 320 million inhabitants—over four times its population at the beginning of the present century. Ten gigantic super-metropolitan areas will contain 107 million people—one-third of the nation's population [and equal to the entire U.S. population in 1920]. Another 40 per cent of the American people will reside in about 285 metropolitan areas having populations between 100,000 and 5,000,000. Cities and urban areas of smaller size will contain about one-half of the remaining population. Urbanites will compose about 85 per cent of our national population.

These figures mean that not only will there be a great many more people living in our country, but our society will have become far more urbanized even than today. "The city, with its diversity of people, its complex economic, social, and physical structure, its dependence upon all parts of the national economy, its need for transportation (both internal and external), and its vitality of growth, will dominate every section of the country." The monograph predicts a geographic expansion of the city in the next forty years of 55,000 square miles of additional land surrounding the metropolitan centers, assuming each square mile accommodates 2,500 people. This is an area approximately equal to that of the entire state of Illinois, roughly 2 per cent of the entire land area of the United States.

The following table offers a comparison of the ten largest metropolitan areas in the United States in 1910, 1956, and (projected) 2000:

TEN LARGEST METROPOLISES, UNITED STATES,
1910, 1956, and 2000
(Population data in millions)

1910 CENSUS Metropolitan Area	Pop.	1956 ESTIMATE Metropolitan Area	Pop.	2000 PROJECTION Super-Metropolitan Area	Pop.
New York	6.7	New York	14.0	New York	23
Chicago	2.5	Los Angeles	5.8	Los Angeles	20
Philadelphia	2.0	Chicago	5.6	Chicago	11
Boston	1.6	Philadelphia	3.8	Detroit	9½
Pittsburgh	1.0	Detroit	3.4	Chesapeake and	
St. Louis	0.8	San Francisco-		Potomac	9½
San Francisco-		Oakland	2.6	Delaware Valley	8½
Oakland	0.7	Boston	2.5	San Francisco Bay	7½
Baltimore	0.7	Washington	1.9	S. E. Florida	6½
Cleveland	0.6	Pittsburgh	1.7	New England	6½
Cincinnati	0.6	St. Louis	1.7	Cuyahoga Valley	5
TOTAL	17.2	TOTAL	43.0	TOTAL	107½
% of U.S.	19 %	% of U.S.	26 %	% of U.S.	33 %

The percentages at the bottom of the chart give the most reveal-ing statistic. In 2000, one-third of the country's population may live in only ten "super-metropolises." It is also interesting to note that such areas are developing outside of the traditionally metro-politan northeast; in fact, three of these "new" metropolitan areas —Los Angeles, Detroit, and southeast Florida (Miami-Palm Beach) —will be among the top ten by 2000. Take note also that this chart assumes that a number of "mergers" will take place—simply because of geographical expansion and overlapping. Thus Wash-ington and Baltimore will form a single super-metropolis and move up to fifth place, while Cleveland will take in Lorain, Elyria, and Akron to form the Cuyahoga Valley metropolis. Some older, estab-lished large cities, even though taking in a much larger territory, will drop down in the standings—(e.g., Boston-New England, and Philadelphia-Delaware Valley).

These, then, are the prospects for metropolitanization in our country:

> By the end of the century, the United States will possess at least five super-metropoli which will have the general complexity and geographic extent of the present-day metropolitan area of New York. The term "megalopolitan area" may well become a term to describe these future vast agglomerated metropoli, all of which will have grown together by the merging of two or more important centers.

THE IMPACT OF URBANIZATION

The process described above is far more than a set of statistics, such as one might arrive at by studying the migration habits of birds. Human beings are involved, therefore social relationships. For them, the shift from rural to urban society is far more than a geographic dislocation—it is a change in the way of life, a change of work, values, and relationships. Sociologists Harold L. Wilensky and Charles N. Lebeaux provide us with an admirable study of the effects of urbanization, and it is from their *Industrial Society and Social Welfare* that the following summary analysis is drawn. All of the consequences of urbanization listed below constitute a shift from "Who You Are" to "What You Can Do."

1. An increase in job specialization. "It has been estimated that there are thirty thousand different occupations in the United States today . . . ; the *Dictionary of Occupational Titles* gives definitions of more than twenty thousand. These lists show astonishing specialization. In the baking industry one can make a living as a cracker breaker, meringue spreader, a pie stripper, or pan dumper. In the slaughter and meat-packing industry one can specialize as a large stock scalper, belly shaver, crotch buster, gut snatcher, gut sorter, snout puller, ear cutter, eyelid remover, stomach washer (sometimes called belly pumper), hindlegs toenail puller, frontlegs toenail puller, and oxtail washer." [3]

2. A dilution of occupational skills. The skilled craftsman begins to disappear and the work talents of men become more and more like the interchangeable parts of a vast machine.

3. The combination of these first two factors results in an obsolescence of traditional occupational skills, in turn necessitating physical or social mobility or both.

4. Accompanying mobility, the tremendous upheavals in old patterns of family life, e.g., the working mother.

5. The influence of the city reaches out into the rural areas, drawing ever-increasing numbers into the urban society.

6. The development of entirely new occupations and skills to accommodate the complexity of urban society.

7. The consequent rise to dominance of the middle class in the total society, borne out by the following statistics:

[3] Harold L. Wilensky and Charles N. Lebeaux, *Industrial Society and Social Welfare* (New York: Russell Sage Foundation, 1958), p. 59.

UNITED STATES CIVILIAN LABOR FORCE[4]		
	1910 (36 million)	1956 (64 million)
Manual Labor	37.4%	38.9%
Farm	30.7%	9.8%
White Collar	15.1%	30.0%
Service	9.6%	11.6%
Proprietors, Officials, Managers	7.2%	9.8%

8. The growth of large corporations.

9. Finally, as part of the new technology, the advent of automa-tion, which looms as one of the most important factors in the urban socio-economic scene.

The above summary comprises a list of factors "from the out-side" that affect a person's life as a result of, or at least in associa-tion with, the process of urbanization. In other words, an individual has very little to say about whether he shall be touched by any of these progressive influences; they are, at least to his own mind, beyond his control. Thus it is easy to see that "secondary group relationships" become more and more important in his life. And this fact, in turn, affects the social mold. Social analysts in our time have observed a typical pattern of tendencies in the "urban way of life":

1. Secondary contacts increase and spread.

2. Social tolerance and blasé attitudes become widespread.

3. Secondary control becomes dominant.

4. Private interest groups and voluntary associations (lodges, etc.) multiply.

[4] *Ibid.,* p. 92.

5. Social life becomes atomized; the individual stands apart, loses a sense of participation, becomes susceptible to manipulation.[5]

The above summaries only skim the surface of what sociologists and other observers have discovered about the effects of urbanization upon our society. Many studies are available—and it might even be said that *any* serious sociological work today deals at least in part with this important subject. However, we must take a closer look at the component parts of the city itself.

TYPES OF CITIES AND NEIGHBORHOODS

Just as no two people are exactly alike in every respect, so it is with cities and each part of a city—each has its "personality," its distinctive characteristics. It doesn't take a trained academician to discover this fact, but I am constantly amazed and dismayed at how often this simple axiom is overlooked by even some of the most "successful" city pastors. Such a man assumes that since he has had "success" in a certain type of area, all other pastors in the same kind of situation should have similar success using the same methods. But the situations only *look* similar.

Nevertheless, some general categories of cities under various headings can be useful, if only to give a hint of the diversity. For example, classifying cities under the heading of "employment" (economic classification), can result in a list of seven types of city.[6]

1. *Manufacturing.* In manufacturing cities, employment in manufacturing businesses is 50 per cent or more of aggregate employment, while employment in retail trade is less than 30

_____
[5] *Ibid.,* pp. 117-120.

[6] This list is based on Victor Jones' and Andrew Colliver's "Economic Classification of Cities and Metropolitan Areas," in *The Municipal Yearbook, 1960,* Orin F. Nolting and David S. Arnold, eds. (The International City Managers' Association [Chicago, 1960]), pp. 71-73. Data used here is based on censuses of businesses and manufactures conducted periodically by the federal government.

per cent (e.g., Bethlehem, Pa., with 82 per cent in manufactures, only 12 per cent in retail trade). In 1954 there were 403 cities in this category.

2. *Industrial.* In industrial cities, the dominance of manufacturing concerns is offset by a substantial retail trade—the manufacturing ratio is still over 50 per cent, but retail trade is over 30 per cent of aggregate employment. Lawrence, Mass.; Port Arthur, Texas; Wilkes-Barre, Pa.; Decatur, Ill.; and Greensboro, N. C.; are among the 91 cities of this type.

3. *Diversified Manufacturing.* Here manufacturing is predominant but less than 50 per cent of the aggregate employment, and retail trade is second in importance. There are 186 of these cities, including the central cities of Boston, Minneapolis, and Los Angeles.

4. *Diversified Retail.* In this type, retail trade is predominant and manufacturing provides between 20 and 50 per cent of employment. New Orleans and San Francisco are among the 264 cities in this category.

5. *Retail.* If the number employed in retail trade is greater than in any other category, and employment in manufacturing is less than 20 per cent, the city is classified as a retail trade center. Washington, D. C., and Sacramento, Calif., are the largest cities of this type; there are 248 in all.

6. *Wholesale.* In wholesale cities, the number employed in wholesale trade is at least 25 per cent of the aggregate employment. Only eight independent cities are of this type, including Columbia, Mo., and Fargo, N. D.

7. *Service Centers.* Twenty-two cities with over 30 per cent of their workers in service establishments are classified as service cities. Several can be recognized as resort and amusement cities,

like Atlantic City, N. J., and Reno, Nev. Others may be service centers for surrounding mining and agricultural areas. A few are residential suburbs, such as Piedmont, Calif., and Richmond Heights, Mo., where service employment is relatively high only because of the absence of manufacturing and trade establishments.

There are, of course, other ways to classify cities, and even within the above classification several of the cities mentioned have secondary tags such as "government," "transportation," "resort," or "education," where there is relatively high employment of *residents only* in these fields.

When it comes to classifying *neighborhoods,* there is an even wider assortment of classifications and categories, and the uniqueness of the "individual" becomes even more apparent. Only a few examples of neighborhood types can be given here: that which is populated primarily by the young adult, single, unattached, office worker; the "beatnik" settlement; the "Gold Coast," which often takes form in upper-income citadels; the high-rise public housing compound; the intellectual neighborhood, which may border on the Irish Catholic colony, which in turn may be adjacent to the Polish settlement (though miles removed psychologically).

Obviously a responsible churchman who wishes to communicate the gospel in a certain area should know as much as possible about the character of the neighborhood and the city in which it lies. In addition, he should be aware of the fact that the urban setting is anything but static. Perhaps the neighborhood is becoming a haven for senior citizens, or perhaps a large number of people fleeing from broken homes are moving into the area. Or the neighborhood may be in the process of becoming a new home for the Jewish population. Another area, which has long been primarily the domain of a particular ethnic group, may see that group scatter to the outer rim of the city. In some instances, a strong institution—a major corporation, a university, a hospital—will provide the focal point for a whole new urban renewal project.

The urban ministry should be thoroughly aware of the extremely fluid and dynamic quality of its setting. Much of the difficulty we are in today is due to the fact that we were not aware of what was going on around us in the past few decades—an era during which churches that once stood in open countryside became surrounded by areas officially designated as slums. And where nothing even faintly urban existed thirty years ago, today there stand the suburbs and many of our churches.

AN IMAGE OF ONE CITY

Without any intention of using it as a "model," it would be helpful at this point to take a closer look at just one of these living organisms we call "the city." For some years Detroit has been under systematic study by a group of social scientists at the University of Michigan, under the direction of Dr. Harry Sharp; their project is known as the Detroit Area Study.[7] At last year's annual meeting of the Religious Research Association, Dr. Sharp presented a summary of some of the group's interesting and pertinent findings, and I review these here with his permission:

An important characteristic of large urban communities the world over is that the growth of their population has almost always been much more dependent upon in-migration than upon "natural increase." Detroit is no exception: of all residents of Greater Detroit who are of voting age, only about 30 per cent are native-born residents of the community; the rest have moved into the area from some other community. Of these in-migrants, a decided majority of those born in this country come from the northern part of the United States. A rather large minority (about one-fourth) of the in-migrants were born on farms; Negroes es-

[7] A Lutheran colleague, Dr. Gerhard Lenski, has been a part of this project since its inception, and has written of religion in Detroit from the study's findings. *The Religious Factor* (New York: Doubleday and Company, Inc., 1961).

pecially are likely to have had a rural background, usually in the South. About two out of five Negro in-migrants are rural-southern by birth, compared with one out of twenty whites. A situation such as this necessarily gives rise to problems of adjustment, since the differences in social organization between the rural South and the urban North are so great—but the problems arise to a certain extent wherever there are differences between origin and destination.

Forty years ago and more, the problems arising out of in-migration were largely a matter of foreign-born people moving in with an "indigenous" population and encountering problems in adjusting to their new surroundings. Since 1920, however, foreign-born Detroit residents have formed an increasingly smaller proportion of the community's total population, due to the tightening of U.S. immigration quotas and to the growth of the total population through natural increase and native in-migration. This kind of adjustment, which has been romanticized in our novels and popular culture, is far less problematic than it used to be. Whereas in 1920, 30 per cent of the population was foreign-born, today the figure is only 15 per cent, and most of the foreign-born are concentrated in a few ethnic groups. Social and economic distinctions that used to mark ethnic and nationality groups in almost direct proportion to their percentages of foreign-born are disappearing, especially among people under thirty-five.

Today the romanticism of *Abie's Irish Rose* and *East Side, West Side* must be set aside in order to discover what problems the native in-migrants face. Differences in community of origin would be of only passing interest if these differences were not associated with other demographic, socio-economic, and behavioral variations between in-migrants and old residents and among the in-migrants themselves. For example, in-migrants tend to shy away from such voluntary organizations as the Masons or neighborhood social clubs, which attract older residents, though this generalization does not apply to church or labor union membership. But, after five years or so in a community, the in-migrant becomes integrated rather quickly into voluntary groups and also begins to exercise his voting franchise. This integration occurs much more quickly with northern in-migrants than with those from the South, who are considerably younger and are clustered in considerably lower socio-economic groups than the northerners.

Other statistics from the Detroit Area Study show the importance of the geographical location of a church in relation to the people it wishes to serve. About half of Detroit's churchgoers spend no more than ten minutes on their journey from home to church, and only one out of every four spends as much as twenty-five minutes. Well over half of the churchgoers live within two miles of their church, and 40 per cent live within one mile. Thus it can be seen that relatively few Detroiters who move from one neighborhood to another will continue to attend the old church. The high mobility within the city is shown by the fact that approximately one half of the church members have been members of their present congregation for no longer than five years.

Once again, only a sketchy idea of the actual situation can be obtained from such a brief presentation of data. Nevertheless, what has been given should be enough assurance that the title of this lecture, "The Urban Upheaval," is no misnomer.

CITY PLANNING AND URBAN RENEWAL

There was a time when anything resembling the title of this section would have been thought unnecessary interference with the individual's freedom of action. Today official planning agencies are, on the whole, an accepted part of the urban scene, and are even helping to *protect* freedom of action for many individuals. At any rate, in the light of the flux and change of today's cities there is no question that they are necessary; therefore, there are "914 cities [that] have some sort of official planning agency. . . .

Almost one-third of the cities with planning agencies have full-time directors."[8]

Not only have the numbers of these agencies increased (so not only the great metropolitan centers seem to be concerned with planning and renewal), but the types of agencies have become more diversified. All these agencies are not municipal; planning is carried on at the levels of the metropolitan area, the county, the region, and the state. These agencies attempt to make comprehensive analyses of population trends, shifting land usage, etc., and to apply the results of their analyses in action and long-range planning. Their activities are seldom carried on in secret, and there is no reason why forward-looking churchmen should not avail themselves of the information they have or acquaint themselves with their goals. Church jurisdictional units, such as synods or districts, should also acquaint themselves with the over-all plans for their areas. Urban renewal also plays an increasingly significant role in American life.

> Fifty-one slum clearance and urban renewal projects were approved during 1959 bringing the total of federally assisted projects at the end of the year to 699. These projects are located in 417 communities, a net increase of 31 over those participating at the end of 1958.[9]

By the end of 1960, 475 communities had some clearance and urban renewal projects either completed or under way and the total number of such projects now stands at 870.

To be eligible for certain kinds of federal support, a community must formulate its own "workable program" for housing and urban renewal, which is then examined by the Housing and Home Finance administrator. To merit approval, a program must be directed toward the following objectives:

[8] Mary McLean, "Planning and Zoning—Developments in 1959," Nolting and Arnold, eds., op. cit., p. 278.
[9] John D. Lange, "Housing and Urban Renewal—Developments in 1959," ibid., pp. 314-316. The data which follows is from this article.

adequate local codes and ordinances, effectively enforced; a comprehensive plan for development of the community; analysis of blighted neighborhoods to determine treatment needed; adequate administrative organization to carry out urban renewal programs; ability to meet financial requirements; responsibility for rehousing adequately families displaced by urban renewal or other governmental activities; and citizen participation.

Under this setup, "A total of 321 communities submitted workable programs which were approved by the administrator during 1959, bringing the total at the end of the year to 1,056."

Public housing is another area in which federal assistance is given. "During 1959, 179 localities applied to the Public Housing Administration for federally assisted, low-rent housing numbering 29,904 dwelling units. . . . The total number of dwelling units in the programs under Public Housing Administration jurisdiction at the end of 1959 was 585,212. Of this total, 464,915 are completed and under management, 24,202 under construction, and 96,095 in the preconstruction stage."

Urban areas are being transformed before our eyes—there is no denying this. Countless thousands are moving out to suburbia and being replaced by untold numbers of new urban in-migrants; vast neighborhoods are decaying; and here and there gleaming new structures rise above the grime and confusion of the city. The latter are almost invariably the result of urban renewal and planning. The church cannot be in the dark about such movements. If it is to have a ministry in the city at all, it must take part in and be sensitive to the tremendous value conflicts inherent in urban renewal, facing such questions as: Where shall we renew? How shall we renew? For whom shall we renew? A recent study points up these conflicts:

> The objectives of an urban renewal project will often represent a choice between competing alternatives, each of which is backed by worthy motives. In every city, there may be a few areas where

the renewal opportunities are obvious, and the choice is relatively simple. It becomes much more difficult as a city's program probes deeper into the "grey area." If the experts make the decisions on objectives behind closed doors, they are acting at their own risk because later on they will need the understanding and support of the community in carrying out their plans. . . . The community should understand that an urban renewal project can eliminate obnoxious conditions, but urban renewal in itself does not eliminate the motivation that produced those conditions.[10]

CONCURRENT POLITICAL QUESTIONS

"What to do about the cities" has always been an important political question in our country. Once again we must discard the romanticism of the past, the semi-humorous images of ward heelers, flunkies, and machine politics in general. Not that these no longer exist—they certainly do. Nevertheless there is a new kind of city politician on the scene, the man who is interested in active urban renewal and is concerned that the city not die from within. These politicians are raising pointed questions which show the crucial nature of politics in the whole matter of urban upheaval.

For example, the former mayor of Milwaukee, Frank P. Zeidler, is concerned about the clash between cities and the up-state and down-state voters:

A condition of increased hostility may result. . . . Since rural and suburban voters may likely total the largest bloc, such a division will also increase the chances of the taking away from the urban areas of their proper representation in state legislatures. Also there will develop permanently in state constitutions the system which in Wisconsin is called the "Area-cat" form of government—namely, that form in which area rather than people is represented in the state legislature.

I also look in this decade for increased state concern for some

[10] Martin Millspaugh, "Objectives and Criteria of Urban Renewal," *The Urban Problems,* Thomas J. Peardon, ed. (New York: The Academy of Political Science, Columbia University [May, 1960]), p. 53.

suburban areas in opposition to the central cities. This will occur largely because some suburbanites will have considered their status and life improved to the point that they will . . . vote for . . . conservatism and status quo. . . . Legislation directed against the development and improvement of the urban centers will often be sponsored by wealthy suburbanites who make their living in the central area.[11]

Top planners are much aware of these political problems that are already raising themselves in the urban picture—men like Martin Meyerson, director of the Joint Center for Urban Studies at Harvard and M.I.T.:

> Will citizens persist in their present reluctance to allocate personal income to local taxes for public services? . . . How consumers decide to allocate their income will have critical importance for the metropolis. . . . Since the end of World War II all indications have been that the consumer, as voter, often refuses to subject himself to further taxation even for the services he wishes.

> How will the political identification of citizens in the suburbs and center cities change as the communities change? How will local political parties alter? As the center-city resident moves to the suburbs and becomes a property owner, he commonly shifts his allegiance to what he regards as the party of property. Will that pattern continue, and if it does, will the subtle status and other distinctions . . . persist? Or will possible deterioration of his property, high taxes, and poor services lead him instead to what he regards as the party of protest?[12]

Naturally the church cannot identify itself with a party or its ideology. Nevertheless it must be aware of the political side of the urban upheaval, and be willing to take a courageous stand on political issues that affect the people to whom it wishes to min-

---

[11] Frank P. Zeidler, "Urbanism and Government, 1957-1977," *Metropolis in Ferment* (Philadelphia: The Annals of the American Academy of Political and Social Science [November, 1957], pp. 76-77.

[12] Martin Meyerson and Barbara Terrett, "Metropolis Lost, Metropolis Regained," *ibid.,* pp. 7-8.

ister. This may mean siding with one party against another, so utmost precaution should be taken that identification is not made. Individual churchmen should be actively concerned with politics, but the church's only concern is to offer all men the opportunity of oneness in Christ.

2

CLASS AND CASTE

Undoubtedly the largest problem of "class and caste" in our contemporary society is the "racial question." Everyone should know by now the crucial nature of this problem, its bearing on national and international politics, its status as *the* moral issue with which our country must concern itself.

It is also a "moral issue" for the church, although this is too weak a terminology. Fortunately, an ever-growing number of clergymen and laymen are bearing witness to the position that the church must serve all men and it proclaims a Christ who is Lord of all, regardless of color or class. At the same time, more than a few of our churchmen maintain that there ought to be separate churches for the different population groups. However, these lectures are concerned not with the racial question as such— there have been some fine books written on this from a Christian viewpoint—but with the church's responsibility toward *all* the population groups that exist in the urban setting. Since, as we shall see, the problem of the inner city is becoming more and more the problem of the Negro, then one must raise the question of whether the church's mission in the city includes working with and for the Negro in helping him to secure better job opportunities, freedom of residence, and so forth. Fortunately, a positive answer to this question is gaining wider and wider assent. If the church is to work for justice for all, then the Negro should be its particular concern, he who has so often been shortchanged in matters of justice.

Unfortunately, in many areas of the church there is considerable lack of understanding of the scope and depth of the problems of class and caste. I hope this lecture will contribute to a better understanding of racial and cultural problems, at least as they are found in metropolitan areas. It is my firm conviction that the responsible Christian in this country must not only seek to win the Negro into the fellowship of Christ's church but must also study, work, and pray that the Negro may have equal opportunities in all areas of life.

THE POPULATION PICTURE

It is in the large metropolitan areas where the issue of racial change is of such importance in our day: the fourteen major areas that have over a million inhabitants. Not that racial change is not taking place elsewhere, but situations in smaller areas lack the complexity and magnitude of racial change in the metropolis. It is these larger areas that attract the largest number of Negro newcomers from the South, a group which has perhaps the greatest transition to make from rural to urban society.

Economic factors seem to play the most important role in bringing Negro in-migrants to the city and thereby increasing the ratio of nonwhites to whites in the city proper. The Negro goes where jobs are available; in our present economy, to the large industrial complexes in the cities. They settle in the city proper, since the suburbs, in most cases, are beyond their reach socially and financially. So it is no surprise that the percentage increase in Negro population in the central cities of our larger metropolitan areas is so great. The following chart documents this trend:

PERCENTAGE INCREASE IN POPULATION OF NONWHITES		
Metropolitan Area	1940-1950	1950-1960
Baltimore	35.9	45.1
Boston	68.6	58.9
Buffalo	106.2	92.9
Chicago	80.5	65.0
Cleveland	76.1	70.0
Detroit	101.4	60.5
Los Angeles	116.2	95.6
Minneapolis-St. Paul	53.0	76.2
New York	62.4	45.2
Philadelphia	49.9	40.9
Pittsburgh	32.9	22.4
St. Louis	41.4	39.7
San Francisco-Oakland	198.0	71.1
Washington, D. C.	50.5	46.6

The 1960 census has shown that with few exceptions the actual population of cities (that is, within the city limits) has changed little in the past decades. The expansion of population has definitely taken place in the suburbs. Thus, as white city residents flee in increasing numbers to the suburbs and more and more Negro in-migrants move into the central cities, the ratio of Negroes to whites has increased drastically. Washington, D. C., became according to the most recent census, the first American city in which Negro residents outnumber white residents; the more than 400,000 Negroes there make up 54 per cent of the population. In 1950, the 280,000 Washington Negroes comprised 35.4 per cent of the total population—an increase of well over 100,000 and almost twenty percentage points in only ten years!

Other cities show the same trend, though to a less degree. Baltimore in 1950 had 225,000 Negroes comprising 23.8 per cent of the population; today 327,000 Negroes make up almost 35 per cent of the city's inhabitants. In 1940 Chicago was 92 per cent white; by 1950 only 81 per cent, with almost 500,000 Negro residents; in the 1960 census over 800,000 Negroes comprise 23 per cent of the city's population; and a study by the University of Chicago indicates that by 1970 Negroes will make up one-third of the population of our second largest city. Similar forecasts are made for New York City, which, though it has the largest Negro population (over a million) still has a situation in which only 14 per cent of the population is Negro. Nevertheless, officials there estimate that by 1970 Negroes and Puerto Ricans together will constitute 45 per cent of the population of Manhattan, and almost one-third of the entire city.[1]

Unless some radical and unforeseen changes occur in present trends, evidence indicates that by about 1980 Negroes will comprise from 25 to 50 per cent of the population in at least ten of our largest cities. What does this imply for the nature and scope of the church's concern and involvement in the next twenty years? At the present time we are relatively weak in the central cities and strong in the rural and suburban areas. But by 1975 an estimated 70 per cent of our nation's population will be in metropolitan areas. Certainly it would seem that those church members in the outlying areas should become informed about and involved in the struggle for racial equality and adequate services for all classes and groups of people—or it will be too late.

This would apply to the suburban church member as much as to the rural church member. Very few suburbs have experienced the kind of racial change going on in the central cities, and if the present patterns are maintained they are not likely to. But the suburban areas are part of the metropolitan complex, and their

---

[1] The figures in this section and the preceding chart are taken from the 1960 U.S. Census Bureau statistics published by the *Chicago Tribune,* March 15, 1961, and from the *1950 Census of Population,* Vol. 11 (States), U.S. Bureau of the Census.

residents must eventually come to understand that their own situations are closely tied in with those of the central city.

THE NEGRO IN THE CENTRAL CITY

Although it is the primary source, in-migration from the South is not the only factor involved in the increasing Negro population; it is a fact that, at least in the cities, natural increase of nonwhites has a much higher rate than that of whites. Nevertheless, the in-migration process shows no signs of decreasing; in fact, it is likely to increase because of dissatisfaction in the South in the wake of the Supreme Court's decision on segregation and the holding policies of white southerners. In addition, as the in-migrant communities in northern cities become larger, there is more appeal to a southern Negro to join his relatively well-established relatives and former neighbors in the north. One factor which might possibly slow down Negro out-migration from the South would be rapid industrialization and urbanization in the South. In some areas there are signs of this happening, but in the main it would seem to be something for the distant future.[2]

Within the northern cities themselves there is a fairly consistent pattern of residential distribution and expansion of the Negro population; the word for this pattern is "segregation." In all major cities with a significant Negro population there exists a "black belt," or a series of "black areas." In Chicago, for example, 79 per cent of all Negro residents in 1950 were living in census tracts in which at least 75 per cent of the residents were Negro, while 84 per cent of the non-Negroes were living in census tracts in which less than 1 per cent of the residents were Negro.[3]

[2] This possibility was raised by Philip Hammer, an economist, in his report to the Conference on the Lutheran Church in the South of Tomorrow, held at Atlanta in September, 1960. An excellent series of papers from this important conference is available from the Division of American Missions of the National Lutheran Council, 327 S. LaSalle St., Chicago 4, Illinois, for $1.00.

[3] Otis D. Duncan and Beverly Duncan, *The Negro Population of Chicago* (Chicago: University of Chicago Press, 1957), p. 96.

It seems that once a neighborhood begins to "change," to shift from predominantly white to predominantly Negro occupancy, the change is never reversed. To a very small degree some of the postwar programs of public housing and urban renewal have managed to buck this trend, e.g., the Lake Meadows project in Chicago's South Side, but these are definite exceptions. Even in public housing projects, usually when such a project is under-taken in a predominantly Negro area what happens is simply the exchange of one Negro population group for another.

As anyone with the slightest acquaintance with urban sociology knows, Negro areas are originally located near the center of the city and gradually spread out toward the city limits. When the time comes for this spreading out (when the saturation point is reached in the already Negro area), the Negroes generally will move into what already are the most mobile neighborhoods, oc-cupied by a non-Negro population with roughly comparable characteristics as the incoming Negro population (in such factors as education, income, etc.).

What of the non-Negroes in a "threatened" area? What are their attitudes toward the impending in-migration of Negroes into their neighborhoods? In the past, the immediate reaction was to flee outward to the city limits and beyond, but there are signs that an increasing number of whites are more ready to accept Negroes as neighbors—some under any conditions at all. Quite a few will remain where they are if a relatively small number of Negroes moves into the neighborhood, but after a "tipping point"—which varies from city to city—is reached, will move out. A recent study takes a more sympathetic view of the non-Negro in this situation than is usual among those currently concerned with race problems:

> The people of the conservation areas, no doubt, generally took it for granted that dark-skinned people were their inferiors. But to a significant extent, what was called "race prejudice" was really dis-like of certain characteristics which were associated with lower-

class people—not only lower-class Negroes, but lower-class whites as well. The prejudice of the people in conservation areas probably included the following components: a) fear of criminals, b) dislike of people who were dirty and disorderly in public places, c) dislike of people with whom they could not readily communicate, and resentment that these people should replace as neighbors other people with whom they could readily communicate, d) dislike of people of lower social status, e) dislike of people of different customs, manners, and ways of dress and speech, f) dislike of people of different physical type, g) dislike of people of different skin color.[4]

Exactly how the "tipping point" operates has been the object of exploration not only of social scientists, but of many others, including real estate operators. Attracted by the higher revenues that come with Negro overcrowding, some of them actually work hard toward the goal of "tipping a neighborhood," without any regard for the possibilities of a truly integrated neighborhood that might evolve if "panic" is not promoted. One social scientist has observed the effect this "tipping-point" phenomenon has on public housing projects set up on an interracial basis, where public housing officials have come to realize that whites will remain in such a project so long as nonwhites do not exceed "roughly 20 per cent of the total residents."

One method used to combat the process of tipping public housing has been to raise rents. This has the effect of decreasing the number of Negroes who can afford to live in the projects. So the tip point leads to a shifting of public housing goals, subordinating the first principle of low rentals to that of maintaining interracial occupancy.[5]

From just the information presented here it can be seen how complex is the racial problem as it affects the urban setting. Also, it can be seen how large a part education—a special education—must play if attitudes between races are to be changed and prej-

[4] Martin Meyerson and Edward C. Banfield, *Politics, Planning and the Public Interest* (Glencoe, Ill.: The Free Press, 1955), p. 103.

[5] Morton Grodzins, *The Metropolitan Area as a Racial Problem* (Pittsburgh: The University of Pittsburgh Press, 1958), p. 7.

udices that stand in the way of equal opportunities for all people are to be destroyed. Christian churches can serve both society and their Lord by taking part in such education, which must, I fear, be first of all an interior process. We must show our people that a Christian's responsibility includes such apparently mundane things as taking a stand for "open occupancy" (which simply means that a person should have freedom to live where he wants), and helping to promote and further tolerance and the maintenance of wholesome communities through responsible community organization. The need for such action is obvious, and there is no question in my mind that it falls into the category of Christian social responsibility.[6]

THE NEGRO AND THE SUBURBS

Obviously the economic factor alone excludes Negroes from most suburban areas; they simply cannot afford the kind of housing that is available in these areas. And undoubtedly there is some truth in the utterances of those who say that most of the Negro inner-city population prefers anyway to remain in its own neighborhoods rather than move into interracial suburban homes, even if they could afford it. Whether this is the case, the real issue is whether the Negro has the *freedom* to make this choice when he is financially capable of doing so. He does not; actually, our suburbs exclude the Negro by many means—legal, illegal, and extra-legal.

Perhaps the attitudes of white suburbanites are not too much different from those of inner-city whites when it comes to this problem, but the suburban community has not only a hostile attitude but also *power*. It has the power to control zoning, building regulations, and subdivisions, and thus maintains its exclusive

[6] For an illuminating discussion of this whole area, see Kyle Haselden's excellent book, *The Racial Problem in Christian Perspective.*

policies by legal means. Where this is not enough, "land use controls are used informally—and of course illegally—to exclude Negroes."

> A Philadelphia builder recently told an interviewer that he would very much like to sell suburban houses to Negroes, but that it was impossible because it would ruin him economically. "If I sold just one suburban home to a Negro, the local building inspectors would have me moving pipes three-eighths of an inch every afternoon in every one of the places I was building; and moving a pipe three-eighths of an inch is mighty expensive if you have to do it in concrete." [7]

And, of course, there is always the cry that goes up about the influx of Negroes bringing about a decrease in property values, which gets the mortgage bankers into the effort to perpetuate the pattern of discrimination. A recent study by Luigi Laurenti gives the lie to this "axiom," incidentally. According to his study, "non-white entry alone—as distinguished from such changes in physical use as increased density—rarely causes residential property to fall in price, and quite often causes it to rise." [8]

Much more could be said about this problem, on the psychological, socio-economic, and political consequences of racial discrimination, but it must remain unsaid here. Much has been written on the subject, and it is readily available to the person who feels that part of his concern as a responsible Christian is to acquaint himself with the situation so that he might act intelligently.

CHANGING ATTITUDES

Far more important than any legislation or judiciary decision against discrimination, in the possible solution of the racial problem, is the fact that people's attitudes can be changed. Attitudes

[7] Grodzins, op. cit., p. 8.
[8] Review of Anthony Downs' *Property Values and Land* (Berkeley, California: University of California Press, 1960), in *Land Economics*, XXXVI, No. 2 (May, 1960), p. 181.

are of great importance to the social scientist, especially one concerned with the city, for an investigation of them can give him and his associate, the community worker, advance notice of changes occurring or about to occur in the social structure of a community.

For example, the Detroit Area Study (mentioned in chapter 1) has discovered important attitudinal trends. In 1951, 54 per cent of white Detroit residents were opposed to school integration in their city. But only five years later, in 1956, 56 per cent of the white residents were *in favor* of complete integration in the schools, while only about one-third remained absolutely opposed. Breaking down these figures it was discovered that southern white in-migrants to Detroit were considerably less likely to be for integration than were non-southern Detroiters, but even among them there was nothing like unanimity. Four out of every ten ex-southern whites believed that schools should be integrated in Detroit, and less than a majority favored segregation. Breaking down these figures further shows the remarkable influence of education on attitudes. More than 60 per cent of the ex-southerners who had at least a high school education (usually in the South!) were in favor of integrating the schools, while less than one-fourth of those who did not graduate from high school were in favor of it. Education also had an effect on northern Detroiters' attitudes, but not nearly to that extent.

Once again, in 1958, the Detroit Area Study polled white residents on school integration. This time 62 per cent were in complete support of integration—not only in Detroit, but everywhere. This means that seven years showed a change of attitude among 18 per cent of the population.

THE CHURCH AND THE NEGRO

A rapidly growing number of congregations of the major Protestant groups in America are integrating and opening their doors to the non-Caucasian. Dr. Karl Hertz of Wittenberg University, Springfield, Ohio, who has been working on a related analysis in the Effective City Church Study of the National Council of Churches, will have some interesting findings to report. Tentatively, he indicates that those persons within any given congregation who are more prone to a "pietistic-fundamentalist" orientation are also more inclined to resist the assimilation of new cultural groups into the membership. He further reports that in the process of transition the "harmony" level or level of "satisfaction" in a congregation tends to drop appreciably. But, he adds, as the transition is accomplished and the crisis weathered, these levels or indices begin to rise again.

Dr. Phillip Hammond of Yale University, in his study of the Congregational Christian churches which made use of basically similar instruments as those used for the NCC project, reports several interesting findings. He indicates that those members for whom religion is the most salient and the most relevant in their lives are least affected by crisis situations in their congregations. Further, according to the research data it appears that being confronted by a transition crisis in the inner-city congregation often deepens the faith of the individuals involved, and that a significant percentage of members begin to find a greater relevancy in their faith.

There are no clear-cut, easy guides to assimilating new cultural or racial groups into an inner-city congregation. However, one very definite need is being pointed up by the preceding research, that of "special" education for both pastors and laymen. Inner-city churchmen need help in redefining the role of the church and themselves in it; somehow they must learn how to make the church's message relevant in their unique situation. This means that if they are confronted by a question of the assimilation of a particular cultural group they must be able to understand the background, the characteristics, and the special needs of these groups.

Such education cannot really be taught as an academic subject; it must arise out of an intensive, searching self-study process, so the congregation can understand both itself and its shifting community.

STORE-FRONT CHURCHES

What of the Negro himself, and other low-income in-migrants from the South? What is their religious situation when they arrive in the city? The first picture that comes to mind is that of the store-front church, the one-church denomination that meets to worship in a way that we who are so completely removed from this cultural level find peculiar. To my knowledge, very little, if any, adequate research has been done on these churches. But they perform important functions for both the white and Negro inner-city dweller, especially the relatively new arrivals. In a sense they provide a bridge between rural folkways and the emerging sophisticated urban society that surrounds these people.

It has been said that the store-front church testifies to the fact that old-line Protestant churches have by and large neglected this population group, and in a sense this is true. But it is not the whole story. Many people who attend store-front churches would be uncomfortable and ill at ease in a more traditional church. So perhaps it is up to Protestantism to find ways of adapting its programming and structuring as well as the level of abstraction in its communication of the gospel to this particular population group. Either that, or simply admit that we are unable to reach these people.

Almost the only statistics available in this area come from the Detroit study, which shows that only 5 per cent of Detroit's Negroes belong to a "Protestant" sect. The same study shows that less than 5 per cent are members of the Roman Catholic church. This is another area for which we have few available statistics, but it is certainly clear that where Negroes have now moved into areas that were formerly Italian, Irish, or Polish, the Roman Catholic church in those areas has suffered drastic drops in attendance. One thing at least is clear: we should not close our eyes to one of the most rapidly growing and highly potential mission fields in mid-century America unless we consider ourselves ineligible for work in the inner-city.

THE GOLD COAST

Before leaving the subject of class and caste, we should look briefly at a somewhat different problem in the area of cultural differences, which nevertheless has to do with the inner city. Last year a major study undertaken by our office in the Central Area of Chicago revealed facts about Lutheranism in this country which have long been suspected but rarely documented. One is, our denomination has as much difficulty reaching out to the upper strata of our society as it has with the lower. Our study revealed that less than one-half of 1 per cent of the population of Chicago's core area (within a four-mile radius of the Loop) are members of the Lutheran church, in spite of the fact that Lutheranism is the strongest Protestant denomination in the Chicago metropolitan area, with six out of every one hundred residents on its rolls. Within this core area are the high-rise luxury apartments of the Gold Coast community on the Near North Side. This elite section has a median income of well in excess of $10,000 per household. Our study also showed that less than 25 per cent of these residents call themselves church members, indicating that Lutheranism is not the only denomination that has difficulty with the extremes of our economic ladder.[9]

As part of the total study we hired a market research firm to

⁹ *Lutheran Central Area Study of Chicago* (the office of Urban Church Planning of the National Lutheran Council, August, 1960).

make a depth analysis of the Near North Side population group to discover something about the background of these people, their past relationships with churches, their interests and involvements in the community, and so forth. Such procedures are necessary if we are to have any idea how to go about contacting people with whom we have completely lost touch. Preliminary findings reveal that people in this class are interested in a "noninvolvement church." Commitment is somehow an offense to the highly sophisticated and cultured orientation of many of them. It is interesting to note in this respect that part of the high cost these residents pay for their exclusive apartments is intended to provide privacy. Even the Fuller Brush man and the census taker have an extremely difficult time doing their jobs in these apartment dwellings.

Our findings in this area are as yet incomplete, but obviously we are up against not only a heritage of neglect but also very real barriers erected by the people themselves. It is a difficult task to attempt to carry the church's mission to this population group, just as it is (for other reasons) to carry it to Negroes and lower-class groups. Unfortunately, too often our pastors and churchmen take the path of least resistance in a desire for numerical growth and quick, tangible success, with the result that whole segments of our society are forgotten in the shuffle.

3

ISSUES FACING PROTESTANTISM

Having taken a look at several of the facts and complexities of metropolitan development and some of the consequences of these in the fields of racial and cultural relations, we now turn to an examination of some of the issues that particularly confront Protestantism in the urban setting.

ULTIMATE VS. PROXIMATE GOALS

It appears to me that Lutheranism, in the midst of its continuing emphasis on theological study and doctrinal correctness, has often been guilty of ignoring what might be called proximate or short-term goals. This is not to imply that the pursuit of theological studies ought to be curtailed, but rather that in the midst of our delineation and analysis of these ultimate and abiding concerns we must have proper appreciation for the more specific, short-term, close-at-hand goals.

Let me illustrate. No one will argue with the statement that our church's primary task is to preach the Word and administer the sacraments. More than a few, however, *will* argue with the suggestion that a congregation ought to make a thorough study of its community and attempt to understand changes that are occurring within its parish area. But this is a short-term goal which in many instances is absolutely necessary so this primary task may be implemented in a given situation. Relating this to theological education, there is a danger that we emphasize the biblical, historical,

and theological studies (all of which are necessary) in our seminaries to the point that little or no attention is given to training
the future clergy in developing an understanding and appreciation
of vital community programs and resources which can be an invaluable aid to urban pastors and their congregations in achieving
their ultimate goals.

Recently I heard criticism of some parish education material
of a certain denomination because it did not seem to have enough
of a Christ-centered message. This particular material dealt specifically with inner-city neighborhoods, and was attempting to
foster a better understanding and a greater mutual acceptance
among children of diverse cultural and racial backgrounds. One
of the ultimate purposes, obviously, was to enable the redeeming
gospel to be proclaimed and the witness to be kept alive in the
midst of difficult and heterogeneous situations. A proximate goal,
no doubt, was to foster an amenable relationship between these
different groups. Without contact and communication between
persons and groups there can be little evangelism.

Many of our urban pastors and congregations must be made
free from their self-imposed restrictiveness as to the nature of their
mission so they can creatively and intelligently respond to specific
situations by applying proximate goals that are evangelically defined
and motivated.

CONFRONTING THE PROBLEMS

Many urban churches are surrounded by and involved in a host
of community problems and their consequences. Not all churches
are aware of these problems; in fact, it is amazing how many
problems are somehow blotted out of the field of vision of both
pastors and laymen. The frequent attempts to avoid or postpone
facing up to imminent problems is unwise and unhealthy for congregational effectiveness. At the other extreme we find those pas-

tors and church leaders who want to "hit it head on," "call a spade a spade," or "be absolutely frank." Such harsh and precipitous handling of problematical situations often magnifies them and creates a series of unfortunate consequences.

In brief, what I wish to emphasize is that there *are* problems and particular challenges that confront the urban church generally and individual congregations specifically. Over and above these, however, we have the additional problem of *how* to confront problems. In other words, problems are compounded by the wrong approach.

I recall one pastor who felt that the best way to deal with his congregational situation, in a neighborhood that would probably change its racial composition within the next five years, was to totally ignore the fact of community change. In his own words, "The longer we can preserve the illusion of strength and stability, the better off we will be when the time comes." Rather than prepare his people by helping them to understand the inclusiveness of the Christian church and the implications of the fact that Christ died for all men, he chose to avoid any reference to the significant community transitions and their long-range consequences.

At the other end of the continuum I have run into those men of the cloth who implicitly, if not explicitly, assume that the "rightness" of their goals somehow automatically sanctifies all of their actions. Unfortunately these are sometimes men who find it difficult to love their fellow man (or themselves), and who delight in having a "sanctified club" with which to hit people. I'm not pleading for gradualism, nor am I merely saying "all things in moderation," which is often roughly translated as the great "middle-of-the-road position." But it is important that the pastor who is in the midst of leading his congregation through difficult times and decisions see himself as the shepherd of the flock, as one who will *help* his people to walk The Way with him.

Perhaps my comments might be interpreted as a rejection of

the workings of the Holy Spirit. Be assured this is not so. I have seen wonderful things happen in the work of the church in the midst of this changing urban frontier, things that could be explained in no other way than that the Holy Spirit had accomplished them. What I am suggesting, however, is that there are certain roles that urban pastors take upon themselves which quite definitely help or hinder our churches in their response to this emerging mission field.

I recall the pastor (and he is not unique) who felt, in all honesty and sincerity, that it was not his role as the pastor of a congregation in a changing inner-city neighborhood to take a stand on a relocation issue facing this congregation. In this particular situation the congregation was planning to relocate and move out of a field of service that definitely needed its ministry. The pastor consistently took the position of "no position"—as though this gave a certain kind of objectivity or purity to his leadership. Obviously what happened was that prevailing social pressures and the trend of social mobility dictated the relocation of the congregation rather than any biblically grounded, doctrinally directed conviction that "this is what the Lord requires of us."

To my knowledge there is no congregation that on its own has withstood these great social pressures and trends and decided heroically to buck the trends, unless it has had courageous, committed, and convinced pastoral leadership. Committed lay leadership is also a must, however. Though a few rare pastors have been able to stand alone in the face of overwhelming odds, it is certainly desirable to have at least a nucleus of staunchly committed lay leadership.

USE OF COMMUNITY RESOURCES

Urban congregations must learn to differentiate between problems with which they alone must cope, and those which are the concern of other institutions in the community as well and can only be dealt with in a cooperative effort. The intelligent use of available community resources is certainly part of an adequate approach to problems.

Tensions between disciplines sometimes present very real difficulties, however. Different frames of reference and different "jargon" may be obstacles to effective cooperation. Social workers and pastors often find it difficult to communicate; likewise, researchers and church administrators encounter communication barriers. In addition, denominational executives are too often considered by local congregations merely as men who have "ready answers" for all situations, rather than as men who can help local congregations work toward solutions of their own problems. Unfortunately there are still a few church leaders who prefer to operate in this "quick answer" framework.

As was indicated in earlier chapters, there are numerous resources available in nearly all communities which can help our urban congregations to better understand their situations, and can even suggest possible programs for meeting the needs of particular population groups. It seems to me that one of the "proximate" goals in every metropolitan area should be for the Lutheran churches, or better yet the Protestant churches, to schedule periodic meetings featuring key community leaders who would bring them up to date on recent developments in the various special fields of interest in the different neighborhoods. Two examples of this, although there are many others, are the Detroit and Milwaukee seminars. The Detroit Seminar was sponsored by the Detroit Council of Churches and the National Lutheran Council, in conjunction with the University of Michigan, in 1957-1958. The Milwaukee Seminar was conducted in 1960 by the University of Wisconsin, in consultation with the three major faiths of the metropolitan area.

Why shouldn't representatives of Protestant congregations in a given neighborhood get together to study, discuss, and develop a planning process for dealing with various neighborhood problems? Some problems are obviously best dealt with on a metropolitan area level, but many can only be undertaken at the neighborhood level, unless metropolitan planning and official action in urban renewal are involved.

THE DIDACTIC VS. THE PROCESS ORIENTATION

Closely related to the matter of the handling of problems and their solutions is the matter of how one goes about it. Churchmen often fail to realize that an inherent part of their frame of reference or viewpoint is the didactic orientation. By this I mean that pastors are often prone to think in terms of "I have the truth and I am about to communicate this to you." This orientation, in its extreme, runs into real difficulties in the changing inner-city neighborhood.

There are *no* clear-cut answers or hard and fast rules as to how a congregation in a changing neighborhood shall go about developing its response to its neighborhood. True, there are overarching principles or ultimate goals, but when it comes to the matter of helping our people in these congregations become redirected in their thinking to arrive at a new definition of the role of their church, then there are many gray zones and many uncertainties. Certain programs may be tried for a while and then scrapped. Perhaps others are launched, later adapted, still later expanded into major emphases of the congregation. In some cases, long established groups or activities of a congregation must be brought under close scrutiny, and prayerfully but resolutely terminated. Whatever decisions are arrived at in the midst of the fluid and dynamic mission field of the inner city, it is important that there be a continuous participation in a process of planning within congregations and across congregational lines.

Perry Norton of the American Institute of Planners, consultant to the National Council of Churches of Christ in the U.S.A., has provided this outline of the planning process:

1. Gather pertinent data and information;

2. Evaluate and analyze the information and experiences;

3. Project probable courses of events in the light of the new understanding of a situation;

4. On the basis of this, set approximate goals and policies;

5. These are examined in the framework of potential action programs which will serve the purposes of these goals;

6. Move from the finalized goals and policies into the effectuation or implementation phase;

7. Examine the whole process by feeding back the experiences gained through these action programs.[1]

Leadership that is oriented to this kind of process is desperately needed at all levels in today's church as it confronts the urban challenge.

CONGREGATIONAL AUTONOMY

The problem of congregational autonomy is of varying import among the different Protestant denominations. I question very seriously whether urban America can be adequately ministered to within the framework of complete congregational autonomy. Just as communities and regions are coming to see the desperate need for over-all planning and co-ordination, so the Protestant church, both within and among denominations, must move in this direction.

The problem of congregational autonomy is of such importance

---

[1] Perry Norton, "The Growth and Nature of the Planning Process" (mimeographed by the Department of the Urban Church, National Council of the Churches of Christ in the U.S.A., New York), p. 11.

to the Lutheran church in this country that it was the subject of a special paper prepared for study by the Committee on Social Trends of the National Lutheran Council. Dr. William Lazareth contributed a section on theological background; Dr. Theodore Tappert wrote briefly on the history of Lutheran polity; Dr. Gerhard Lenski, a sociologist, dealt with the dynamics of community change; and I documented some of the operational or administrative concerns. This paper gives the best summary of the problem that I know of:

> Though essentially one . . . , the Church is both a religious organism and a social organization. As the Body of Christ it can only be believed; as the Lutheran Church it may be structured with any polity which does not belie its nature or thwart its mission.
>
> 1. No congregation should act so autonomously that it destroys the Church's apostolicity.
>
> 2. No church body should act so heteronomously that it destroys the congregations' catholicity.
>
> 3. Any polity may be employed by the Lutheran Church which expedites the proclamation of the Gospel and which implements the exercise of the priesthood of all believers . . .
>
> Lutherans have repeatedly adapted forms of organization to the circumstances of changing times and places. It deserves to be underscored that concern to restore "historic forms," whether from the apostolic or later ages, is alien to Lutheranism, partly, to begin with, because there have actually been *many* historic forms and not merely one; partly because each of these forms was an accommodation to specific circumstances which may no longer exist and represented a borrowing of contemporary "secular" structures and titles; and partly because it has been uniformly stated that the purpose of any polity must be related to the present and not to the past: *the most effective possible framework within which the Church's mission may be accomplished in our time.* [Italics mine.][2]

[2] William H. Lazareth, Theodore G. Tappert, Gerhard E. Lenski, and Walter Kloetzli, *Congregationalism as a Problem in the Exercise of Christian Social Responsibility Within American Protestantism* (Chicago: Division of American Missions, National Lutheran Council).

For nearly two generations the various Lutheran denominations in Detroit sold approximately one inner-city church per year and left their neighborhoods. It is a well-known fact that, in some neighborhoods, overlapping and competing Lutheran congregations are slowly but surely destroying their effectiveness in a community. Still other urban churches remain as monuments to a long-since vanished cultural group of yesteryear in the midst of a tragically urgent inner-city mission field.

Can we continue to shrug our shoulders and say, "Well, the congregation is autonomous—nothing can be done"?

In my opinion, the whole urban upheaval and the increasing interdependence of neighborhoods (even between suburbia and the inner city), makes it imperative that all congregations see themselves in relation to the total Christian witness in their metropolitan area. Those who speak much of being One in Christ too often give the lie to this proclamation by insisting that their congregation can do precisely as it jolly well pleases—regardless of denominational strategy, regardless of responsible denominational stewardship.

Extreme congregational autonomy is not the polity which will provide "the most effective framework" for the church's mission in urban America.

SELF-AWARENESS AND THE CONGREGATIONAL IMAGE

It is not enough that urban congregations merely deal with given problems as they crop up. There must be both foresight and hindsight. Responsible urban church leadership must recognize the tremendous inertia of the rural Protestant image, which for so long has been the accepted conception of our church, and the fact that in the majority of our urban churches a "rural" understanding of the congregation's role still shapes and directs the policy and programming today.

In a sensē we could say that we have in this matter of self-awareness another instance of the ultimate *vs.* proximate goal issue. This particular facet can be labeled the "congregational *image.*" Some of the studies conducted by Dr. Charles Y. Glock[3] in the Effective City Church Study of the National Council of the Churches of Christ in the U.S.A. have indicated that there tends to be a stereotype or traditional pattern which many church members impose upon their pastor and upon the work of the congregation itself.

Forums, study groups, self studies, speeches by community leaders, participation in community affairs, retreats, etc., can be used by urban congregations to help their members become aware that they and their churches have a role that is unique at their given location at this given moment.

Some of the most effective new responses to changing city neighborhoods have emerged from situations in which the pastor and some of his key leaders were quite aware of the out-dated image that pervaded their congregation. Then these men set about deliberately, through theological and community study, to reshape the image of their congregation more in keeping with the evangelical witness relevant to their situation—not as it might or should have been shaped in the rural hinterland some two generations ago, but as it had to be shaped in their situation at that particular moment.

All such changes, of course, demand of the pastor a certain sensitivity to the attitudes and backgrounds of the people in his congregation and in the community. A host of interacting forces and influences are at work in any given congregation, the sum total of which is the congregation as it sees itself and as it develops in response to what it thinks it ought to be. The pastor who

[3] Charles Y. Glock, "A Sociologist Looks at the Parish Church," Afterword to Walter Kloetzli's *The City Church—Death or Renewal* (Philadelphia: Muhlenberg Press, 1961).

accepts as part of his responsibility the updating and reshaping of his congregation's image will find that such a procedure bears fruit.

Before leaving the matter of the congregational image, I shall also mention the importance of the image that the *community* has of the congregation. Every urban church would do well to learn, in so far as possible, what the community thinks of it. Is it considered a significant force in the community? Is it considered a church for only a select group of people? Is it a church that is felt to care for the people of the community and strive to minister to the total man, or rather to open its doors merely one or two days a week and then be closed up tight the rest of the time? These reactions can be quite helpful.

Self-study programs and community polls need not be highly scientific studies—what is needed above all is honesty and a humble and prayerful willingness to examine the congregation. Of course, there are basic techniques to master. One doesn't want to begin an interview by saying, "I'm Mr. Smith from Grace Lutheran Church. What do you think of our church?" It is far more helpful to get a group of people from some church outside of your neighborhood to come in and make inquiries such as, "I'm new in the neighborhood here, what can you tell me about that church down the street?" In this way the replies are more likely to be honest.

UNIVERSALITY OF THE CHURCH VS.
THE IDENTITY OF THE CONGREGATION

Though this issue ties in with image and autonomy, it warrants separate attention. To those of you who have had the privilege of reading Dr. Jaroslav Pelikan's book on Roman Catholicism,[4] the phrase "universality of the church *vs.* identity of the congregation" is readily recognizable. An example of this kind of conflict be-

[4] Jaroslav Pelikan, *The Riddle of Roman Catholicism* (New York and Nashville: Abingdon, 1959).

tween universality and identity is the contrast between the church's claim that it should love all and the fact that the presence of a Negro in a worship service threatens the close relationships within the congregation. At this point many congregations face a real danger of becoming ambivalent and inconsistent. In such cases a pastor will often show his fear of the destruction of the identity of his congregation.

We cannot treat this problem lightly. It is easy to pontificate; it is much more difficult to live through the death of one congregational identity and the birth of another more in keeping with the church's universality. One can quote Matthew 16:25, "For whoever would save his life will lose it, and whoever loses his life for my sake will find it," but it is quite a different matter to experience such transformation. In the midst of constant and continuing change, the urban church faces continuing death and renewal. If the death or loss of congregational identity is done in His Name, then the gift of new life will be provided by Him. Where the old life is protected and preserved at all costs, even to the denial of the "cup of cold water," to some of His children—then there will be death without renewal.

AWARENESS OF CULTURAL DIFFERENCES

Many "liberals" are so anxious to achieve congregational and community heterogeneity that they ignore the very real differences between various groups—and thereby do the church and those groups a real disservice.

At the same time that we confess the universality of the church and our Oneness in Christ, we dare not be blind to the differences of class and culture. It is one thing for a congregation to assimilate into its membership those of different cultural or racial groups from approximately the same class level; it is quite a different matter to accomplish this in the face of extreme class differences. And each group does have its own cultural contribution to make to our society and our churches.

VERTICAL VS. HORIZONTAL RESPONSIBILITY

Roland L. Warren, a social scientist, has elaborated on the "vertical-horizontal conflict" [5] that exists within most institutions. In the case of the urban church he finds this conflict in the clash between denominational loyalty and involvement, and community identification and involvement. It is understandable that in the midst of inner-city tensions many churches revert to an extreme position, generally in the direction of the vertical (denominational) dimension.

If the church is to be a leaven in the community and play a key role in the affairs of society, then there must be the horizontal outreach and dimension as well. Akin to this problem are many others. For example, what shall be the relationship of the witnessing Christian to non-Christians, secularists, etc.? This, of course, leads into the whole discussion of Christian social responsibility, or what is sometimes referred to as "Christ and culture." [6] In the fragmented urban neighborhoods of today it becomes increasingly important that churches work with other key community institutions and agencies to give leadership, cohesion, and substance to the community. Those congregations which are too "vertical," too concerned with denomination association, cannot be as effective an influence in the atomistic, impersonal, urban neighborhood. Relationships and continuing involvements must be established with other key community institutions.

[5] Roland L. Warren, "Toward a Reformulation of Community Theory," *Human Organization*, Vol. 15 (Summer, 1956), 8-11.
[6] See H. Richard Niebuhr's *Christ and Culture* (New York: Harper and Brothers, 1951).

Precisely what this balance between the vertical and horizontal involvements shall be within each congregation has to be developed in each given situation. Some of the top secular leaders in urban communities today are saying that the churches are *the* key institution for stability and spirit in the most problem-torn neighborhoods. Churches have a responsibility to bear witness to the total man—and this certainly includes a witness to and an involvement in the ongoing life of the community.

ECUMENICAL RELATIONS AT THE COMMUNITY LEVEL

In a sense, ecumenical problems are part of the "vertical-horizontal conflict"; yet they go beyond this. Local pastors and church leaders must recognize that the total Protestant witness can be made more effective in a variety of ways. Too many assume that "union services" are the best and only way to cooperate. Conferences and consultations about common problems, opportunities, and plans in the community are certainly necessary ingredients for more effective Protestant witness in urban America.

Then there is the level of coordinated action, and beyond this the level of united action. In all local efforts, whether by individual congregations, groups of congregations from several denominations, or congregations in conjunction with other community institutions, Christians are expected to be found faithful to the gospel and responsible to the Lord of the church.

On the other hand, it should be noted that some congregations or pastors are so "cooperation prone" that they do not adequately evaluate the purposes, methods, and consequences of some community programs to which they give support. In other words, at the same time that I am advocating a greater degree of cooperation and coordination at the local level, I do not propose arbitrary endorsement of all such efforts.

OTHER ISSUES

Certainly other issues confront the urban church. A more complete coverage would call for attention to these issues: how to provide subsidy and help for local congregations without being guilty of paternalism or destroying local initiative; what to do about the rapid turnover of inner city pastors; and what to do about existing relationships and communications between our Lutheran Welfare leaders and agencies on the one hand, and the inner city congregations on the other.

The answers to these problems will be found only as responsible churchmen prayerfully and resolutely go about doing the Lord's business on the various frontiers which they serve in the most informed and creative manner possible. Guiding us in all of our actions should be our Christian calling and our faithfulness to the Lord of the church.

4

ROMAN CATHOLICISM AND
COMMUNITY ORGANIZATION

In this lecture I depart from the pattern of the other four, which are intended to be comprehensive in scope without being thorough in detail, and concentrate on one specific aspect of the urban scene today. Rather than attempt to be comprehensive in dealing with the over-all response of the Roman Catholic church to the urban unheaval and problems of class and caste, I feel I must deal with but one aspect of that response, unfortunately a rather unhealthy aspect, at least to my mind.

In so doing, I must make clear that I do not consider the activities described in this chapter to be typical of urban work carried on by the Roman Catholic church in this country. Like many other Protestants I am appreciative of the positive contributions and the helpful ministries that this church has performed and is performing. To document this attitude would require a book many times the size of these lectures. On the whole, the Protestant can only applaud these endeavors, and compare them ruefully with the relatively weak and tardy efforts of his own denominations to make an effective outreach in the modern city.

Nevertheless, Protestants cannot, in the name of a thin-backboned "toleration," stop at pure adulation of Roman Catholic work in the city. We must be as critical of another church's efforts as we are of our own. And we must also be aware that our differences in theology are very real, and have very real results when they are put into practice.

I concentrate on this aspect of Roman Catholic activity not for the sake of muck-raking (which is the wrong term to use here anyway). It so happens that this is one part of that church's effort that has been receiving a large share of publicity from the public press—not ten, five, or even one year ago, but *today*. It is a strong activity which shows little sign of weakening, and one which has attracted many non-Catholics, including Protestant pastors. Now that controversy has definitely grown up over it, it is regarded as one of the chief problems in urban planning and development today.

THE WOODLAWN CONFLICT[1]

On the front page of the Sunday *Chicago Sun-Times,* dated April 9, 1961, appears a feature article by Ruth Moore with the headline "Woodlawn: Urban Forces in Conflict." It begins, "An urban battle—a war over what a neighborhood, a university, and a city are to be—is raging in the South Side community of Woodlawn."[2] This article is a competent journalistic description of just one incident in which the particular aspect of Roman Catholic urban effort under discussion is a definite factor—as one of the combatants in the "urban battle."

Before analyzing this aspect in detail, let us look at the "Woodlawn Story" as it appears to the informed outside observer. After describing the general area of the Woodlawn community, which borders on the University of Chicago but also includes one of the more blighted areas in the city where crime is a pressing problem, Miss Moore goes on to describe the efforts of the university to launch its plans for the expansion of its "South Campus." This

---

[1] This section's events took place after these lectures were delivered. Because of their pertinence and timeliness, I thought it wise to include this story at the cost of eliminating a portion of the original lecture.

[2] All quotations in this section are from Ruth Moore's articles, and are used by permission.

expansion called for the razing of approximately twenty-eight acres within a strip one mile long and one block wide, and the consequent relocation of the residents of these blocks. The displacement of these residents, who are predominantly low-income Negroes, probably means that certain previously all-white neighborhoods to the south of this area will become the new homes of these relocatees.

But the expansion plans of the university had competition. Before plans were completely formulated, a group known as the Industrial Areas Foundation entered the picture. This was not a newly formed organization; it has been in operation for twenty years, since its inception out of the Back of the Yards area of Chicago. In this area Saul D. Alinsky, executive director of the IAF, first applied the principles of community organization that have since been used in certain cities around the country. Miss Moore indicates that, presumably, for its campaign in the Woodlawn area, the IAF received $50,000 in 1960 from the Roman Catholic archdiocese of Chicago.

The IAF goal, according to statements and actions of its leaders, is to change the historic pattern of Chicago's development: the flight of white populations from areas adjoining the Negro ghetto, the stranding of their churches and institutions, the expansion of the Negro ghetto into the white-vacated area, and the intensification of the segregation of both whites and Negroes.

It is not the goals, but the methods proposed by Alinsky and the IAF for breaking this socially disastrous pattern that have raised the storm. Basically these methods call for:

1. Acceptance of a limited number of carefully chosen Negroes —a quota of possibly 7 or 8 per cent—in the all-white areas abutting the Negro ghetto and the formation of neighborhood "power" organizations to maintain the balance. (This is the frequently attacked quota system in a new guise.)

2. Concomitant measures to "control the population pressures raging without." In practice this often has meant opposition to

urban renewal projects that would uproot either Negroes or foreign-language populations centered around their nationality churches. Both groups are encouraged to stay where they are and improve their areas largely through their own efforts.

With the exception of the minority quotas to be accepted in the areas which formerly barred all Negroes, the IAF program would substantially maintain the status quo by strong controls over real estate and community.

There are those who label the above strategy as "containment and token integration"; that is to say, containment of ghettos and token integration elsewhere. Obviously the South Campus plans would cause dispersal of a ghetto and not containment. Hence, under the guise of "self-determination" and a "people's organization" strong opposition to the university plans was stimulated by the IAF-backed Temporary Woodlawn Organization. The university became a "monster" in the minds of many Woodlawn residents as a result of persistent hate campaigns and scapegoating.

Other groups in Woodlawn became concerned about the things that were happening. "TWO" was giving the impression that *it* spoke for the entire community, and that the entire community was opposed to South Campus. Soon charges and counter-charges began to fly back and forth between TWO and the other Woodlawn groups. The other groups were particularly upset by the declarations of some TWO-IAF directing members to "rub raw the sores of discontent," to arouse "dormant hostilities." These were methods for opposing the university and for preventing community change. As one TWO spokesman said, "We want to keep this a high density, low income community." There was also a memo which stated:

Take up the things that produce resentments and disgust. Show the people how wrongly they are treated. Form them into an organization that will be the most powerful thing in Woodlawn. Only power will defeat unjust power and apathy.

In response to such statements a member of the opposing groups said:

> The fact that a community may be stirred and organized by "sharpening dormant hostilities" and rubbing raw the sores of discontent is not new . . . the technique has been proved in practice in the assembling of lynch mobs. . . .

Three days after Miss Moore's article appeared, describing the situation in Woodlawn, another article under her byline was printed in the *Sun-Times* (April 12) with the headline "5 Pastors Quit Woodlawn Group." The five clergymen, representing four Protestant denominations, withdrew from the Woodlawn Pastors' Alliance, a Roman Catholic-Protestant group which was nominally part of TWO. They made the following statements:

> 1. The alliance and TWO brought in IAF organizers whose "organizing tactics are based on the cultivation of fear, hatred, and usable antagonism."
>
> 2. Spokesmen for the Alliance made statements "in the name of the alliance without the advice or consent of the group"; supported a "demonstration march on 63rd St. without carrying out a promise to consult the group first," and "conveyed the impression at meetings with public officials that the whole alliance was behind the position taken."

It should be pointed out that Protestant ministers serving as presidents of both the alliance and TWO firmly opposed the allegations made by the resigning ministers.

The Woodlawn story is, of course, not finished, and by the time these lectures are published many new developments will have taken place. But the developments there provide us with an ideal introduction for studying Roman Catholic participation in community organization, and the possible reasons behind this participation.

COMMUNITY ORGANIZATION

Before proceeding further, we should have an adequate understanding of the terms being used; terms which are familiar to
anyone involved in the social sciences, but perhaps unfamiliar to
many others. It may seem from the preceding section that "community organization" is evil and to be avoided by responsible persons. On the contrary, we ought to be informed and, where possible, involved in such activity.

> Community organization is a technique for obtaining a consensus
> concerning both the values that are most important for the common
> welfare and the best means of obtaining them [in a given com-
> munity]. The most fundamental values have become so much a
> part of the culture that they are assumed as desirable; they belong
> to established mores. It is the new values which arise out of the
> changing social environment and about which there are diverse
> attitudes that test the strength of community organization and give
> rise to the need for integration.[3]

> Community organization as a process includes not only the ele-
> ments of authority, division of labor, and channels of communica-
> tion as essentials of common action which are generally found in
> communities. Attention is also directed . . . to the growing interest
> in problems of developing leadership and stimulating participation;
> the relation of community structures to each other, functionally
> and geographically; and the possibility of agreement on means and
> ends. . . . While communities have always been organized informally,
> more definite and conscious methods of establishing patterns of
> cooperation are necessary and possible under modern conditions.
> This last is important, since the informal organization is often
> nothing more than a consensus that the status quo should be
> maintained.[4]

Community organization is of various kinds, as can be seen from

[3] D. Sanderson and R. Polson, *Rural Community Organization* (New York:
John Wiley and Sons, Inc., 1939), pp. 5-6.

[4] Arthur Hillman, *Community Organization and Planning* (New York:
Macmillan, 1950), p. 14.

the broad definitions provided. The diversity and importance of community organization can be seen from the story of Woodlawn, in which no less than four groups can be classified as examples of community organization. The only way to distinguish them is to discover the motives for their being formed, then to understand what their goals really are.

URBAN RENEWAL

We must also understand the term "Urban Renewal," in spite of the glowing connotations that may have been associated with it. This has a specific definition: it is a federally-aided program including local action which seeks to bring about the rehabilitation of neighborhoods and the physical improvement of cities generally.

Obviously, when buildings are torn down to make way for some new structures, or when expressways cut through neighborhoods (not, strictly speaking, urban renewal), many people are displaced. "Relocation" is the word used to designate the process whereby people from older residences are enabled through local relocation agencies to secure other living quarters, and this has been called the Achilles heel of urban renewal. There is no question that the relocation practices of our cities could stand a great deal of improvement.

Relocation is not the only corollary of urban renewal that has been criticized. There are also the architectural monstrosities that some of these programs produce, causing families with small children to live in twenty-story brick towers looming over the urban landscape. Another criticism is that renewal reduces the population in inner-city neighborhoods, whereas some say the density should actually be increased to curtail displacement and mobility.

Many of these criticisms are undoubtedly well taken, but it must be remembered that urban renewal is still relatively new on the urban scene, and much of it is still conducted on a trial-and-error basis. Professional planners, municipal and federal agencies have much to learn, but the burden of mistakes does not lie completely with them. In a way, the renewed community, with whatever shortcomings it might have, is the end product of many of our contemporary value judgments and reflects the political realities of the community.

THE ROMAN CATHOLIC CHURCH
IN THE INNER CITY

In a sense the problems which face the Roman Catholic church in the inner city are those which also face the Protestant church and which already have been documented in these lectures. It is difficult to create for our suburban-oriented minds all of the dynamics and innuendos of inner-city neighborhoods—one has to work in them for some time to get even a vague idea of all the factors involved. Nevertheless I hope that the first three lectures have given some idea of the inner city, without which it is impossible to differentiate between present separate and special problems to each of the major Christian denominations.

The special problems of Protestantism have already been described; they are primarily a matter of being unaware of the crucial situation in which the urban church finds itself, although even among those who have this awareness there is too often an attitude which is rather helpless. This is the assumption that everything—ghettos, the location of public housing projects, city renewal, and so forth—is "given," and that there is really not much the church can do about them. We will see that this assumption is certainly not held by many Roman Catholic clergy involved in the urban upheaval.

But the Roman Catholic church has very real problems in the inner city, and has been hit harder by changing neighborhoods and mobility than most Protestants suspect. We are so prone to think of the inner city as a Roman Catholic stronghold, centering in various ethnic groups and overshadowing the feeble minority of Protestants, that we do not appreciate that this is no longer the case. The old ethnic colonies and nationality ghettos are breaking up—some more rapidly than others—and are rapidly disappearing. Second- and third-generation descendants of the foreign-born in our cities become increasingly Americanized and tend to move away into more heterogeneous communities (at least in terms of ethnic and religious, if not economic, background).

Not all Catholic parishes are formed on a geographical basis, as we often assume—especially in the inner city, where the numerous nationality parishes tend to overlap geographical boundaries. Thus, when members of a nationality group began to desert the general area in which their church stood, and when they also began to lose their identity as a nationality group, the church which had served them suddenly found itself without a parish, in terms of human beings. One of the big problems the Catholic church faces in our time is the fact that those who move into such an area have had little or no contact with and therefore show little interest in Roman Catholicism.

More often than not, the new group coming into such an area is predominantly Negro. Where this is the case there is an additional complication, for the process described above does not happen in so "natural" a manner. The out-migration of old parishioners is precipitated by the very fact that Negroes were moving into or threatening to move into the neighborhood. As a Roman Catholic priest in Chicago said, "Whenever the Negro tide has rolled over an entire neighborhood with lightning-like speed it has reduced the parish congregation to a tenth of its former size almost overnight. Ninety-four per cent of the Negro people are not Catholic."[5]

---

[5] From a speech by the Rev. Patrick Curran, quoted by Ruth Moore in "Woodlawn: Urban Forces in Conflict," Sunday *Chicago Sun-Times* (April 9, 1961), p. 36.

According to figures presented at a Roman Catholic conference in Chicago, "by 1960, 76 Catholic parishes, or nearly one-fourth of those in the diocese, had experienced a heavy in-movement of Negroes." [6]

At this point it is noted that the Catholic church, because of factors in its basic theology, cannot take the easy way out which is available to Protestant congregations—that is, to pick up stakes and follow its people wherever they have moved. It is almost impossible to do this once the building and the property on which the church stands have been consecrated to the service of the church. (There is, of course, no prohibition against building an entirely new parish church in the area to which people have moved.) Faced with this problem in a neighborhood already changed, the church often embarks on an energetic program to convert the Negro. But where the problem only threatens, here the reaction is often quite different.

In this situation, the Roman Catholic church in some of our cities has turned to a particular type of community organization in an effort to control the transition of neighborhoods and thereby moderate the losses of parish membership that occur in changed neighborhoods. This effort is generally a co-operative venture, involving community leaders and Protestant church leaders in the particular neighborhood being threatened, and often the effort has been co-ordinated by the Industrial Areas Foundation—not accidentally, but with the support, financial and otherwise, of the local diocese.

THE INDUSTRIAL AREAS FOUNDATION

The IAF and its executive director, Saul D. Alinsky, have already been mentioned. In certain circles this organization is quite well

[6] Ruth Moore, op. cit.

known, and it makes no secret of its guiding principles, its scope of activity, and its goals; Alinsky has written a book, has testified before the U.S. Commission on Civil Rights, and talks freely in press interviews. Nevertheless, the general public, along with most Protestant church workers, are only vaguely aware of the IAF until they come into direct contact with it.

The IAF grew out of the Back of the Yards Neighborhood Council in the area of Chicago south and west of the stockyards, as has been indicated. The organization attempted there was successful in reducing mobility and preventing the neighborhood from changing. The council succeeded in aligning labor unions, Roman Catholic parishes, businessmen, nationality groups, a few non-Catholic churches, and organizations, in its original co-operative effort. "The actual interests and achievements of the Council are not essentially different from similar organizations. . . . The intangible by-products of co-operation between groups whose interests are otherwise divergent or hostile to each other is sometimes claimed as outranking in importance any specific achievements. There is also stress on the method of action backed by a powerful alignment of people, as compared with the approach of the liberal, the social worker, or the 'do-gooder' who talks and surveys a situation to death. A rather frank defense of opportunism in tactics is included as part of a 'radical' [referring to Alinsky's book, *Reveille for Radicals*] approach to a sick community situation. This emphasis has been criticized as being merely a sophisticated version of the methods of the machine politician or more seriously as a Fascist threat in the disguise of democratic symbolism." [7]

Let us look at this criticism more closely, lest it seem to be hysterical oversimplification. According to Ruth Moore, "Alinsky outspokenly scorns the usual methods of community organizations. He calls for straight political and other direct pressures: registering

[7] Hillman, *op. cit.*, pp. 173-174. Reviews in 1946 of the Alinsky book are cited.

the voters, pressure on City Hall, mass demonstrations, all-out attacks on opponents. It means, Alinsky says, organizing and bargaining like a trade union."[8] Is this in itself a "bad thing"? Here we get into some rather gray borderline situations; after all, I have been urging the church to become involved with its community, and these are all important elements of the community. But the important thing, it seems to me, is the kind of thinking and basic attitude that underlies such techniques. A recent philosophical critique of Alinsky's *Reveille for Radicals* raises that question:

> Here we get the impression that nothing can be accomplished without power. It is claimed or inferred that power can be used for good ends, even though it be built up by deception, by fabricated disputes, by alliances between theistic Christians and atheistic Communists. . . . I believe that [Alinsky] . . . values success and survival too highly. He describes the unhappy, depressed community and shows how this local community cannot exert sufficient pressure to secure public improvements unless the various community groups forget their differences and join forces. But should they forget all their differences? Should a clergyman join forces with a gangster? Are the interests that stretch beyond the local community of no value? Is "togetherness" more important than what we do together?[9]

The major criticism brought against Alinsky's methods is that they seem to operate under the assumption that the end justifies the means, trite as that may sound, and the dispute is between those who would subscribe to that assumption and those who would not.

There is also the question of the ends themselves, not as they are stated but as they actually occur. It is pointed out that in the case of the Back of the Yards neighborhood, segregation has been established and exists to the present day. No Negroes live in the community, though it is close to the center of Chicago and

[8] Moore, *op. cit.*, p. 36.
[9] Wayne A. R. Leys, "Machiavelli in Modern Dress," *The Christian Century* (November 11, 1959), pp. 1308-1309.

close to large concentrations of Negro population. Since that time, as noted in Miss Moore's article, the IAF has modified this kind of goal for interracial problems; it advocates what can only be called a quota system, whereby limited numbers of Negroes (or any group toward which the community is antagonistic) would be permitted to settle in the neighborhood in a sort of token integration.

Alinsky firmly believes, as he testified before a Chicago hearing of the U.S. Commission on Civil Rights in May, 1959, that this is the only method that will effectively prevent the usual pattern of white communities becoming Negro ghettos. He "advocated a possible quota of 5 to 7 per cent for white areas in the way of Negro expansion" and "emphasized that there would have to be an effective control force, a community organization 'with the power to do the job.' "[10] Let us look briefly at how an IAF-organized effort worked in a different part of the country:

The case of Chelsea, a neighborhood in Manhattan which was typically faced by many of the problems of urban upheaval, was well publicized.[11] First, a council was launched which would include the wide variety of interests and agencies already at work in the area. It soon became apparent that council was to have absolute authority over its member agencies. Bitter attacks were made against any organization (such as the Hudson Guild settlement house and the International Ladies Garment Workers union) that blocked the goals of the council, which were primarily intended to "freeze" the community and preserve the status quo. In this particular instance, the largest religious group in a fairly heterogeneous community was the Roman Catholic. This seemed to have been singled out as "the major power group" in the community, and

[10] Moore. loc. cit.

[11] A full report of this incident may be found in the article by Everett C. Parker, "How Chelsea Was Torn Apart," *The Christian Century* (February 3, 1960), pp. 130-133.

became the strongest voice in the council. In the end, the community was split down the middle, the Roman Catholic majority on one side and the various other groups on the other, each blaming the other side for the fiasco.

Much more could be said here about the specific techniques used by the IAF—distorted statements, opposition "planted" to gain public sympathy, and so forth—but this might obscure what I consider to be dangerous about such an organization. The IAF, it should be remembered, appeals to Protestants because it has thrown its support behind some worthy projects and ideas; but often, it seems to observers, only when those projects would serve some other purpose—stop neighborhood change by any available means, on the basis of the thinking that this is the only feasible answer to the situation.

THE IAF AND THE ROMAN CATHOLIC CHURCH

I am not going to offer any legal brief here in an attempt to show a tie-in between the Roman Catholic church and the IAF. In the first place this is unnecessary. The fact that the IAF has received funds from the Roman Catholic church is public knowledge, as is the fact that it is endorsed by the National Conference of Catholic Charities. Besides, many of the Catholic clergy, many of them in inner-city work, have commended the work of IAF and, when community organization is in the discussion stage, have suggested that the IAF be called in. The Catholic church, incidentally, is not alone in its endorsement of Alinsky's foundation; the IAF has received financial support from several non-church groups, as well as support and approval from a wide variety of people, including Protestant ministers. But there is no question that the Roman Catholic church is one of the IAF's most active supporters, and quite often (as in Chelsea) the favor seems to be returned.

It should be obvious now why this is so. Both favor the same goals, although perhaps for different reasons. This is not conjecture on my part. In a recent conference on "The Catholic Church and the Negro" in the Chicago archdiocese, Albert Cardinal Meyer, in his three-point program, recommended to the conference "the establishment of strong community organizations of the type of the IAF-sponsored OSC [Organization for the Southwest Community, a group of the same sort as TWO in Woodlawn]." [12] Msgr. John Egan, director of the Cardinal's Conservation Committee, has said: "To develop democratic citizen participation, to encourage urban renewal and slum clearance programs, and to hasten integration we aid and participate in a wide variety of programs which include: special training of laity and clergy . . . in proven citizen community action programs, such as those begun by the Industrial Areas Foundation. . . ." [13]

I met Msgr. Egan early in 1959; in fact, through him I first became aware of the activities of the IAF. One of our Lutheran pastors in Woodlawn had been in conversation with a local priest and other Protestant pastors. When they agreed that they should be taking drastic measures to improve the community, a meeting was arranged at which Msgr. Egan proposed that the various groups represented should contribute funds over a three-year period for the purpose of organizing the community to enforce zoning, improve physical conditions, etc.—and he knew just the agency to do this work and provide supplementary funds, namely, the Industrial Areas Foundation.

The idea was appealing, as were some of the criticisms leveled against urban renewal programs, but our office first investigated the background of IAF and came across the information I have presented here. We decided we could not support Mr. Alinsky's methods and many of his goals, but made clear that we were still

[12] Moore, *loc. cit.*
[13] *Ibid.*

interested in supporting a broadly based, local community organization in the neighborhood. Some top-flight community organization people submitted dossiers, but as soon as it became clear to Msgr. Egan that we would not support his proposal to bring in the IAF, he lost all interest in the project. Apparently Msgr. Egan's several years of training under Alinsky, during which time he served as research assistant for the Industrial Areas Foundation, had convinced him that no one else could provide the kind of community organization he had in mind for that area. This feeling is supported by an article in which Msgr. Egan says, "The only rehabilitation and conservation program of any size which can honestly be called a success is the one conducted by the Back of the Yards Neighborhood Council in Chicago."[14]

Some Roman Catholic clergymen, including Msgr. Egan, are particularly virulent in their attacks on urban renewal and the accompanying relocation practice. As I have said, some of this criticism is justified, but little that I have seen deserves the excessive and extended criticism that has been leveled.[15]

Undoubtedly there are dedicated men among the Catholic clergy who firmly believe that Alinsky's methods and goals are the only answer to the urban upheaval, and for reasons with which anyone could agree. One cannot help but wonder, though, about the strategy of containment and token integration. Is this the method espoused by an ever-growing number of Catholic dioceses here in America? Many think so. One can understand the fear of having many nearly empty churches in the midst of Negro ghettos. Further, it is understandable that institutional self-interest should suggest the attempt to "freeze" a neighborhood. But are there not higher

[14] *The Ave Maria* (Notre Dame, Indiana: Ave Maria Press [May 10, 1958]).

[15] It is worth noting that the Chicago archdiocese is not supporting publicly its parishioners who are threatened with displacement in the Harrison-Halsted area (proposed site of the University of Illinois). In this case it appears that the Catholic institutional self-interest is better served by supporting (or at least not opposing) this urban renewal project.

values, higher goals, than the success of a few institutions in a community? What of the total welfare of the total metropolitan area? What of the long-term consequences of these actions for the minority group residents who are frozen in or out of various neighborhoods? [16]

All of this seems an unfortunate blotch on the record of the Catholic church in this country; unfortunate because when it comes to racial integration that church has in several instances been ahead of the Protestant churches. Surely they have a dilemma and no one would object to their acting in self-defense. It is at the point of questionable means and devious manipulation of a community that one raises warning signals. I do not oppose the Catholic church for fighting its battles, but I do oppose their forming "front groups" to draw others into their defense.

Involvement in power struggles or politics may be inevitable— but is it the role of the church to initiate conflicts and exploit discontents? Basically, it is evident that the *conflict* method is divisive in the community, as in Chelsea and Woodlawn, and minorities are not protected when power considerations are made paramount. Both objectives and methodology of community action should be subject to scrutiny and judgment based upon the Christian ethic.

ALTERNATIVE COMMUNITY ORGANIZATION

After this extended criticism of one type of community organization, it is essential that guidelines for adequate community organization be provided, so it may be seen that we are not faced with a choice between the IAF or nothing at all. These seven principles are being applied by professional people in the field:

(1) *Community responsibility.* No community within our metropolitan areas is completely lacking in earnest and capable men

[16] A pertinent editorial, "Open or Closed Cities," appeared after these lectures were given. *The Christian Century* (May 10, 1961).

and women who are devoted to the whole people. No community is devoid of civic, religious, and charitable organizations. The destiny of each community is dependent upon the willingness of such leadership to take upon itself the burden and the promise of the community; to cultivate programs of improvement and cooperation which are indigenous to the people concerned, which involve their free and full participation, and which give them a sense of continuity in the changing community; and to seek from beyond the community such aid as is required for the achieving of the community's rightful destiny.

(2) *The right to know.* The people of a community have the right to know what is behind proposals they are called on to endorse and should insist on that right. Whatever is done must be done in the full light of day. "Open covenants openly arrived at" is an essential if good faith is to be maintained. This applies to the functioning of community councils and of all representative bodies, and to staff operations.

(3) *Clear objectives.* Objectives must be democratically arrived at and clearly formulated. The development of community organization as a "power structure" without a clear indication of the purposes for which the alleged power is to be used is an invitation to dictatorship and failure. It takes time to define objectives in this way, but it is time well used, for in the process of defining objectives the organization extends its spiritual roots.

(4) *Checks and balances.* The idea of setting up an all-powerful group within a community organization—a group whose power cannot effectively be challenged—is wrong in principle and destructive in practice. Power corrupts at the community level as well as at the national. Checks and balances have to be set up and a spirit created which will make them work through continuous operation of the principle of consent of the governed and the continuous use of collective bargaining.

(5) *Methods.* The method used in community relationships should and must be consistent with the end desired. The end sought is community development. This requires cultivation of confidence, mutual respect. The tactic of deliberately stirring up community animosities, widening rifts and exaggerating differences

in the interest of so-called power is iniquitous and self-defeating. Churches which refuse to oppose such tactics in the interest of their own imagined advantage betray their mission as churches and are bad corporate citizens.

(6) *Integrity of leadership.* Professional leadership which is presented for employment in these projects must be made up of men and women who are incapable of serving two masters or of subverting the enterprise. The greatest care must be used to make certain that persons entrusted with staff responsibilities shall be mature, possessed of demonstrated personal integrity.

(7) *Institutional integrity.* It is highly important that the principle of pluralism be acknowledged by the churches involved in the project. This means that churches must participate for the benefit of the community and not for their own advantage. The test of whether this principle is accepted is to be found in the composition of the board of directors. No church or denomination should seek or be given a majority of membership in the controlling body.[17]

[17] "Urban Community Organization," *The Christian Century* (March 30, 1960), p. 373.

5

EMERGING PROTESTANT RESPONSES
TO THE URBAN CHALLENGE

I hope I have managed to convey, in the course of the preceding four lectures, that the actual situation of the Protestant churches in the urban settings presents anything but a bright picture today. The history of our churches in the face of the urban challenge does not, for the most part, lend itself to praise, and even today the traditional pattern of discouragement and retreat continues all too frequently. It is with these sobering facts in mind that we raise our heads from the gloom and examine some areas and programs within the church or on its perimeter where healthy and affirmative action *is* being taken.

There is no question in my mind that a new dimension has definitely been added to the urban work of Protestantism in recent years. But if one wishes a list of illustrations which would document "dramatic" experiments and "breakthroughs" in the inner city, startlingly vivid *exempla* of the "new dimension," he is bound to be disappointed. Occasionally one of the actual responses tends to take on a dramatic aura, but the vast majority simply are not material for movie or TV scenarios—they are of a more subtle and undramatic nature, unless one appreciates the drama of the ordinary, the challenge of the commonplace.

There is one dramatic element, of course, in all of these responses. Inevitably there is conflict, an antagonist. The gains that have been made have faced stiff opposition within the urban congregations themselves, where conservatism and resistance to *any* kind of change is often firmly entrenched, where the status quo has been approved and endorsed, where faith has fused with culture, and where stability is held higher on the scale of values than service. And too often those urban congregations that do find themselves "busy" and active are mightily engaged in nothing more than recreating a successful congregation in the image of the accepted business ethic of our time.

Out of the conflict, and in the midst of the resistive and bewildering forces of urban life, there are emerging literally hundreds upon hundreds of transformed congregations and other new inroads of response to the urban challenge. For this fact we can only be thankful to Almighty God, for such response is due largely to prayerful seeking of what the Lord requires of his church and how its members might be found faithful.

It can be seen, therefore, that the primary area in which response must take place is theological—without a firm theological grounding, any response is all too likely to be confused groping. Before examining what has been done in this area, however, one matter should be clarified about the peculiar situation of the inner-city church. We tend to think of modern American culture as being generally sympathetic to the Christian church and, in part, formed by it. We must not be misled—the gospel is an offense wherever it is proclaimed if it is rightly proclaimed, and therefore the task of proclaiming it is difficult at all times and in all places. But we must also recognize that, whereas most of our churches find themselves in communities that are fairly supportive, permissive, and sympathetic (factors that can be subtly dangerous to the right proclamation of the gospel), there are also communities where being a part of the church is not a generally accepted facet of life and where even some of the forms and structures of the church may seem foreign to the community's population. Quite often this is the case of the inner-city community. Here the church itself is on trial in a "crisis situation," and must determine not only how to proclaim the gospel but also how to *survive* to do so. In this respect, numerous inner-city pastors and laymen state, out of deep experience, "Only those churches with a strong theological foundation, a real doctrine of the church, can possibly survive to serve in these extremely difficult neighborhoods."

In a "crisis situation" the church finds itself stripped of any comforts that might be offered by the surrounding society, and examines its very reasons for existence. Out of such examination comes theological revival, or, to put it less abstractly, a new understanding of what the Word of God means to us and to all men as we actually find ourselves.

THEOLOGICAL STUDY

Since these lectures are being delivered to primarily Lutheran audiences it must be pointed out that Lutherans have no reason to be smug or self-satisfied with their historical emphasis on theological correctness. Too often we have been prone to a mistake at the other end of the scale from a too-easy adaptation of our standards to those of society—that is, to a rigid, static, and essentially meaningless insistence upon "correct" doctrine. We are just beginning to learn that the only doctrine that is "correct" is that which is grounded in the Word of God *and* is also dynamically relevant to the specific actual situation.[1]

Among those who have testified in moving language to the effectiveness of thoughtful and searching theological study by congregational groups is Father Kilmer Myers, formerly of St. Augustine's Parish on the Lower East Side of Manhattan and

[1] The *Christian Social Responsibility* series edited by Harold Letts (3 vols.; Philadelphia: Muhlenberg Press, 1957), documents both the history of the Lutheran application of Christian ethics and the current approach.

presently of the Chapel of the Intercession in Harlem. He has written of his work in the densely populated, lower-income neighborhood in Lower Manhattan which has become a home for all kinds of minority groups and today includes thousands and thousands of Puerto Ricans and Negroes. Out of this and earlier experience (in Jersey City) he pleads that the Protestant church place its hope for inner-city work in something other than gimmicks, techniques, or programs.[2] That "something other" should be, he contends, solid theological study groups conducted within the core membership (the most committed members) of the congregation, so that they should know what the doctrines they profess to believe actually mean. Once this group has grasped the true nature, purpose, and mission of the church, it can go out into the community to teach others what it has been taught, and thus become a "leaven" in the community. This leavening process includes not only person-to-person contacts but also a recognition by the church of the various power structures in the community and an exertion of the influence of the representatives of the church of Jesus Christ upon these community structures and programs.

It must be remembered that this implies not that the church *discard* all "programs" in favor of such theological training, but simply that this training be at the heart, at the very nerve center, of any significant response to the urban challenge. Thus, at St. Augustine's there were numerous programs and services rendered by the parish to the community—including a staff of trained social workers, recreational and social activities for youth, etc. And, from personal observation, I should add that I have met very few urban pastors with the sensitivity that Father Myers has to both the psychological and the sociological dynamics of his parish, and with such thorough knowledge of church history, social work, urban

[2] C. Kilmer Myers, *Light the Dark Streets* (Greenwich, Conn.: The Seabury Press, Inc., 1957).

power structures, power politics, institutional images, Communist infiltration techniques, etc.

Let us look, then, at some of the "programs" that have been undertaken.

THEOLOGICAL TRAINING

In the light of what has been said above, it is easy to see that the question of theological education is of utmost importance to us. If ministers and others who seek theological education are not shown the relevancy of their faith to our urban world, then the blind certainly cannot lead the blind. In this as in all other questions pertaining to the work of the church, the institutions of theological education must come in for a major share of criticism and examination. As already noted in an earlier lecture, one of the points made in the Niebuhr study of theological education was the need for helping the seminarian to understand the dynamics and specifics of the emerging urban communities. How many of our seminaries actually provide this help?

Allowing this rhetorical question to go unanswered, we take special note of two programs that have been set up at McCormick Theological Seminary in Chicago. One, entitled "Church and Community" and led by Dr. Charles Chakerian, helps the seminarian to develop a real understanding not only of social problems in the abstract but also of the immediate practical facts about social welfare, community planning, community organization, etc. This program is carried on in co-operation with the universities of Illinois and Chicago, an arrangement whereby the student who wishes to be trained in church-related social work spends a specified period of time at the seminary and the university, thereby obtaining a background in both social welfare and theology. The other program is under Dr. Marshal Scott and is called "Church and

Industry." Here both seminarians and graduate students are enabled to understand some of the theoretical aspects of industrialization and technological change, and also to have first-hand experience on the assembly line and in the industrial labor force. Both programs function at two levels—as part of the student's training and also as an in-service training center for inner-city pastors, parish workers, and social workers.

McCormick is a denominational institution; unfortunately, seminaries of the Lutheran denomination have taken no similar steps to broaden their theological education.[3] Let us hope that we do so before too long. In other areas of response we are doing our part.

TOTAL PROTESTANT PLANNING

Co-operative planning among the Protestant denominations has been a significant area of response in recent years and has received considerable attention. The planning process, the development of a strategy for the churches on the basis of all the available data, has already been discussed in the third lecture, and it should be obvious that it is not only desirable but essential for Protestant groups to work together in such efforts to bear the most effective witness to their confessions in today's urban areas.

Such work has been joined by Lutheran churches throughout the country, and I can mention only a few examples here. In Indianapolis all Lutheran groups are participating in a program of research and planning under the direction of the Rev. Fred Michel. As an outgrowth of the excellent school on the Church and Regional Planning conducted in Detroit in January, 1960

---

[3] The Lutheran Theological Seminary at Gettysburg, Pa., has Dr. Bertha Paulssen as professor of sociology and psychology. Her required and elective courses have enabled students to receive considerable background and understanding in these fields.

(sponsored by the National Council of Churches), a promising program of research and planning has developed in Cleveland. Protestant leaders there have been fortunate in securing the services of a theologically educated and professionally trained city planner, Lyle Schaller. The research and planning program of the Detroit Council of Churches, under the leadership of the Rev. Raleigh Sain, has been rendering valuable service to the Protestant churches for many years in the field of suburban church planning. In 1960 Larry Kersten, a professionally trained city planner, was added to the staff to give specific attention to urban renewal and inner-city neighborhoods.

There is, perhaps, still some reluctance among Lutherans to enter into such co-operative ventures. It is necessary therefore to include here five propositions which were approved by the National Lutheran Council early in 1959, and which pertain to this subject:

1. Recognize that fundamental facts concerning urban growth and adjustment are not matters of doctrinal significance, and therefore that the Lutheran Church can actively participate with other Protestants in securing these facts, and that therefore it can share in budgets and direction of active research in the study of the church growth and adjustment in relation to general urban growth and adjustment.

2. Join with other Protestants in determining Protestant Church needs in relation to urban growth and adjustment, and join with them also in presenting these needs to city and community planners and to housing developers.

3. Develop a formula for determining the need for Lutheran churches and for the responsibility of the Lutheran Church in a metropolitan area in relation to the need and responsibility for other Protestant churches so that the most effective total Protestant witness can be achieved.

4. Recognize that there are significant doctrinal differences between Protestant groups and plan within our own circle and within the Protestant whole so that the Lutheran witness may be repre-

sented in each section of the urban area, including the expanding suburbs. Spacing and distribution of Lutheran churches would be determined by their own comity procedures, but the establishment of these churches would not be undertaken without conference and consultation with other Protestants.

5. Establish a structure for Protestant planning and adjustment through which all plans for new congregations, radical program changes in established churches, and church withdrawals from established fields, would be cleared. The structure should be consultative and advisory rather than regulatory. It should be responsible for establishing norms for adequate churching and interpreting the spiritual wisdom of these norms to the denominations. It should recommend to the denominations strategic adjustments that ought to be made in the light of urban growth and change.[4]

Ten, even five, years ago there were relatively few Lutheran groups willing to take part in co-operative planning. Today the number is rapidly increasing.

GROUP MINISTRY

Before looking at any more of the areas of denomination response, or the variety of techniques that are being used, we will pay homage here to a special type of response that was one of the first kinds of Protestant action to bear fruit in the midst of the urban challenge. This is the group ministry, as found in the East Harlem Protestant Parish and its Cleveland and Chicago counterparts. Numerous accounts of the work of this unique thrust of Protestantism have appeared in books and in *The City Church,* a magazine published by the Department of the Urban Church of the National Council of Churches in New York, as well as

[4] H. Conrad Hoyer and Walter Kloetzli, "Planning Together with Other Protestants" (Chicago: Division of American Missions of the National Lutheran Council, 1959). At that time Dr. Hoyer was executive secretary of the division; at present he is the associate executive secretary of the Division of Home Missions of the National Council of Churches, with specific responsibility for co-operative planning.

in denominational periodicals. In addition, members of the various group ministry staffs have done an excellent job of communicating their work experiences and the fruits of their theological studies through the same media.[5] Therefore I will limit myself to the barest outline of their objectives and procedures.

The New York staff has formulated a statement of purpose for the East Harlem project which gives a rough idea of the area of its activity:

1. To bring the basic Christian gospel to those underprivileged groups of the deteriorated sections of the city among whom for various reasons the conventional church approach has been unsuccessful.

2. To explore methods of personal evangelism and small fellowship groups which may provide new techniques for Christian ministry in underprivileged areas.

3. To provide a training center for seminary students who feel called to missionary service in the disorganized areas of the inner city.[6]

The staff of the East Harlem project consists of two classes of full-time members. First, there are the full members of the group ministry, who are under a serious "discipline," and then there are the probationers, who may be ordained seminary graduates but must nevertheless serve a year in this category before they can be fully inducted. The discipline is fourfold:

1. Economic: "No person on the staff is paid on the basis of seniority or status, or longevity in the Parish" but on the basis of need.

2. Political: The staff acts as a unit; a clear majority is not to be blocked by a dissenting minority. The staff does not directly

[5] One of the recent books to come out of the group ministry effort is George Webber's *God's Colony in Man's World* (New York and Nashville: Abingdon, 1960).
[6] As quoted by Ross W. Sanderson in *The Church Serves the Changing City* (New York: Harper and Brothers, 1955), p. 192.

involve the congregations, except as their support for policies agreed upon by the staff may be sought.

3. Religious: Including weekly Communion and other practices or personal and group observance.

4. Vocational: Individual opportunities for professional service elsewhere are reviewed by the group as a whole. Mutual counsel has proved invaluable as new decisions have become imperative. Members of the group ministry are particularly grateful for the "encouragement, evaluation, and criticism of one another's work at their weekly meetings." [7]

The work of the various group ministries has been underwritten in part by several denominations in each of the cities, in part by interested individuals from outlying neighborhoods, and also by interdenominational funds.

We are grateful for the contributions of these men and women in the group ministries, made on one of the most difficult frontiers of the whole urban complex, but we need not insist that every response of the church conform to their pattern, which was devised for a particular situation at a particular time. The group ministry has been a thorn in the flesh of complacent Protestantism—on the one hand reminding it of the tremendous mission challenge of the inner city, and on the other helping to point the way both theologically and operationally toward a new response to the urban challenge.

NATIONAL MISSION POLICIES

Today very few national mission boards, denominational and interdenominational, are without keen awareness of the urban challenge and many of its implications. And this awareness is not limited to a few specially favored officials who serve on the mission boards; rather it would seem that the church as a whole,

[7] *Ibid.*, pp. 201-202.

at least in its leadership, has gained this awareness. For example, a film recently released by the American Lutheran church, "The Measure of A Man," is intended to portray the various kinds of mission opportunities that face the ALC and it devotes a significant portion of time, at the very beginning of the film, to the church in the inner city and the responsibility of the total church to enable the witness to be maintained and strengthened in such places. The film speaks for the denomination as a whole, which is even more significant when it is recalled that the ALC has a heavily rural background; it is the most "rural" of the larger Lutheran synods.

In the United Lutheran church vast sums of money are now being spent by the national mission board for inner city work. In addition, the denomination has a consulting committee on the urban church, on which sit representatives of all the different boards and commissions of the entire church. Further, within such operations as stewardship, evangelism, parish education, etc., special attention is being given to the uniqueness of the inner city and its implications for the various programs and projects. For example, this recognition of the uniqueness of inner-city situations resulted in the ULC sponsoring a Spanish School for Pastors in New York City in the summer of 1960. About twenty men who serve in neighborhoods with a significant Puerto Rican population underwent an intensive ten-week program during which they talked, read, almost lived Spanish in what amounted to a year's course in college. Similar schools are being considered for other parts of the country.

The national mission boards stand ready to guide, assist, support, and enable (in so far as possible) their congregations in changing neighborhoods—providing, of course, that the congregations have a job to do in that neighborhood and providing that they are really willing to do that job. The boards are aware that some congregations unfortunately look to them as some kind of agency that will enable them to postpone the day of reckoning and to perpetuate the status quo, rather than aid them in breaking through to a new ministry in their communities.

SEMINARS

I mention here just one more type of action that has been taken on a broad or co-operative basis, before going on to the specific parish situation. I have already mentioned the Detroit and Milwaukee seminars in the third lecture; the former was initiated by Lutheran churches and held in conjunction with other Protestant denominations and the university, while the latter was even more ecumenical, where Catholic and Jewish clergymen joined in sponsorship and participation. Comparable seminars are being planned for, among other places, Chicago and Baltimore.

The main contribution of these seminars is to bring together interested clergy and key authorities on a variety of community problems, under the enabling and educationally-oriented administrative leadership of the local university. To give an idea of their scope, I will set down the titles of the topics in the Milwaukee Seminar: "The Milwaukee Metropolitan Community, Problems and Prospects," "The Changing Character of Community Life," "Urban Redevelopment and Its Implications," "An Introduction to Group Process and Decision Making," "Problems of Intercultural and Interracial Relations," "The Changing Pattern of Family Life," "Social Welfare and the Metropolitan Community," "Juvenile Delinquency," "Mental Health and Mental Illness," "Alcoholism," "The Problems of the Aged," "Congregations in a Community: a Case Study," "Congregations and the Community; the Planning Process."

Personally I hope that in every metropolitan area of our nation seminars of this kind will be conducted in the near future—and not just once. Perhaps some of the topics might be changed for the succeeding seminars, and certainly the material would be updated. And, of course, with the mobility of the clergy being comparable to the national population mobility, half the "class" would be new every several years.

SELF-STUDIES

Let us turn now to the resources available to the individual congregation. One of the more widely used aids in the redefining of congregational roles in urban areas has been the self-study program.[8] In the vast majority of cases, these studies have been conducted by Lutheran congregations of an entire metropolitan area. Essentially, the program is intended to assist congregations in their appraisal of themselves and their neighborhoods in order to arrive at a redefinition of their role in their changing situations.

In addition to the benefits derived by local congregations, there have been educational "by-products" coming out of the self-studies, including:

a) a greater awareness and understanding of community problems and available resources;

b) the development of a metropolitan area concept of missions against a strongly parochial orientation;

c) a reappraisal of "success" as the major goal in congregational life;[9]

d) the undergirding of all work with the assurance that the *total* church is concerned and stands ready to render assistance.

[8] Described in detail in Walter Kloetzli and Arthur Hillman's *Urban Church Planning* (Philadelphia: Muhlenberg Press, 1958).
[9] For a stimulating discussion of this value see *Christianity and Crisis* (November 28, 1960 and December 26, 1960).

The next step to be taken with the self-study is to place it in an interdenominational context. Already congregations from coast to coast of the Lutheran church—Missouri Synod have participated. It is essential that if planning is to be done jointly, then self-study should also be on an interdenominational basis.

EVANGELISM

Most church bodies have "departments of evangelism" or similar groups; perhaps more than any other arm of the denomination, the field of evangelism requires special attention when the urban situation is involved. Such departments are beginning to avail themselves of the advice and assistance of those specially qualified for urban work, in an example of the kind of special attention being given the city by the denominations previously mentioned.

In the field of evangelism, there is no substitute for the direct personal confrontation between the believing Christian and the non-church member. However, in the various types of inner-city neighborhoods it becomes necessary to think in terms of the kinds of outreach that are most suitable for the specific circumstances. The telephone (through the use of the reverse directory) can be of considerable help in most inner-city neighborhoods in establishing some contact with the people in the community—except in the case of the lower-income population groups. These latter are naturally skeptical of anyone offering them something over the phone, and only in a few cases will a telephone call pave the way to a personal follow-up call. These people have been so often exploited, over the phone and otherwise, that even when they are familiar with the church building and the denomination, they tend to consider the evangelistic caller just another exploiter.

In other socio-economic groups the telephone has proved useful, especially in the high-rise apartments where no other kind of entree in available (the Gold Coast). Here the only problem is that many barriers still prevent a follow-up to the call. In the broad middle belt of the population telephoning most generally opens some doors for follow-up visits.

Many city churches have attempted some sort of systematic publicizing of their location and programs through the neighborhood press, handbills, posters, direct mailings, etc. These are commendable efforts, so long as they stay within the limits of publicizing and do not fall into the trap of "selling" religion. Such campaigns require considerable work, and seldom do they produce dramatic results, but they are necessary simply to let the population in the highly fluid, transient, and impersonal inner-city neighborhood know that the church exists.

Some churches are holding "cottage meetings" in apartment houses, where member families who are residents invite non-member families in the same building to come to their apartment for an evening of Bible study or theological discussion and fellowship. Not every member can handle such meetings, but often they enable the church to reach individuals who would never have been reached in any other way.

Other churches are attempting to foster adult education programs which in a sense are vocationally and avocationally-oriented evangelism efforts. In this way people who perhaps could not be reached by the usual methods are brought into contact with the church by their interest in art, music, vocations, social action, community problems, and so forth.

PROSPECTS FOR THE FUTURE

At this point it can be said that much of the "flight from the blight" of which Protestantism was guilty has been brought to a standstill. Members, it is true, are still moving out of inner-city neighborhoods and leaving their churches, but at least now our churches, where needed, are staying. And not too long ago our office released a filmstrip showing that in the last forty years almost forty Lutheran churches had moved out from the heart of just one city, Detroit.

It would be foolish here, however, to "point with pride." Grateful as we are for what has been accomplished, we look to the challenges of the future. A definite growth has been taking place in the matter of churchmanship. Just one facet of this, but one that affects all types of churches, is found in the area of membership transfer. Congregations seem to be seeing themselves much more in relationship to one another than they have in the past; instead of each congregation trying selfishly and desperately to hold onto its "own," there is a growing emphasis on the church as a whole, with the individual congregation being a part of the body of Christ, which leads to effective Kingdom strategy and the most effective ministry to the individuals and families involved.

There is still a place in our society for the small congregation with a one-man "staff," but I do not feel that place is in the inner-city situation. It is my opinion that such congregations are going to become less and less the norm in inner cities, with the larger parish—an actual yoking of a group of congregations—emerging in many situations. Such an arrangement would enable the church to develop specialists for the inner city and co-ordinate and central-ize certain functions (it would also be a serious blow to our con-gregational autonomy as we now know it). For example, one central office with a qualified secretary-bookkeeper could handle all administrative work for a group of inner-city congregations, none of which could otherwise afford to employ even part-time help in that capacity. The staff of the larger parish could include a social group worker whose services would be available to each of the component parts or chapels.

Such restructuring of traditional Protestant polity has been attempted with some success in the New York area. The United

Church of Christ has a project on the West Side of Manhattan; the Rev. Archie Hargraves is attempting something along these lines in Brooklyn; and of course Trinity Episcopal Parish in Manhattan is the best known for its efforts in this direction.

Where these larger parishes are not suitable, a more loosely organized group of adjacent urban congregations could be formed into area councils (which might then later evolve into larger parishes), with the same benefits mentioned above. Although it is still too early to evaluate the results, Presbyterians have been working along these lines in New York City and San Francisco.

Many other possible experiments could be mentioned here, but I do emphasize one area in which a great deal of work needs to be done. Somehow we must explore the possibilities of yoking or relating suburban congregations with inner-city congregations, before the two lose all meaningful contact with one another. The metropolitan area is a living unit, and the suburbs are related to the inner city in many ways, whether their residents want to admit it or not. Suburban churches, which generally have a more readily available pool of experienced leaders in various fields, must begin to feel a responsibility for sister congregations in the inner city. There are a few scattered instances of how this is done; in the Chicago area, for example, the suburban Oak Park Presbyterian church not only contributes more than $25,000 annually to the support of inner-city church work, but over fifty of its key lay people are directly involved with the work of inner-city churches.

One final word on the subject of the Protestant response is necessary here. Creativity is not something which is available only to denominational officials or professional workers in the city; many creative responses are being developed by resourceful pastors and lay people in their individual situations, some with commendable success. Unfortunately, many of these people do not realize how great is the need for sharing and communicating the insights they have received from their experiences with other congregations. We need to add greatly to the body of knowledge that we presently have, and therefore I would like to make this a direct plea to all who read these lectures: take it upon yourselves to write up as objectively and analytically as possible the various programs, study groups, and operations that you might know about, whether from your own experiences or from those of another church, and submit these reports to whatever central agency seems appropriate. We must share together the sometimes painful, sometimes fruitful, experiences of inner-city church work.

Type used in this book
Body, 11 on 13 and 10 on 11 Garamond
Display, Garamond
Paper: "RRR" Standard White Antique